THE POLITICS
of the
BASIN

A PERSPECTIVE ON THE
CHURCH AS COMMUNITY

D. Robert Kennedy

**UNIVERSITY
PRESS OF
AMERICA**

Lanham • New York • London

Copyright © 1995 by
University Press of America® Inc.
4720 Boston Way
Lanham, Maryland 20706

3 Henrietta Street
London WC2E 8LU England

Library of Congress Cataloging-in-Publication Data

Kennedy, D. Robert.
The politics of the basin : a perspective on the church as
community / D. Robert Kennedy.
p.   cm.
Includes bibliographical references and index.
1. Church.   2. Christian life.   3. Service (Theology)   4. Foot
washing (Rite)   5. Fellowship—Religious aspects—Christianity.
BV600.2.K415   1994   262—dc20   94–18927 CIP

ISBN 0–8191–9567–7 (cloth : alk. paper)
ISBN 0–8191–9568–5 (pbk. : alk. paper)

The major version of the Holy Bible used in this study is the New
Revised Standard Version. However, in some places a more liberal
paraphrase was used when it was felt it would create greater
understanding for contextual meaning.

DEDICATED

TO

June, my life's partner,
who has taught me much
about community.

CONTENTS

PREFACE

This study, by Dr. Robert Kennedy, on the significance of footwashing for the building of community in the church and family, is long overdue. In fact, it should not be read, shelved, and forgotten, because it broadens the implications of the Upper Room scenario in John 13:2-17. Having given scholarly attention to a tradition not known to many contemporary Christian churches, it has also brought forth some profound spiritual insights which are refreshing as well as challenging to our conceptions of life and power in the church. Dr. Kennedy does not seek to rub our noses in denominational differences, but endeavors to speak to the church from a broad perspective. He discreetly addresses an area that is relational in its focus and that calls us to leave the narrow confines of the Upper Room. In the Upper Room, the footwashing was established as a community building ritual by our Lord and Savior, Jesus Christ Himself, Who invites us to turn to the world with the Gospel of power and transformation (Matthew 28:16-20).

The footwashing model of the Upper Room is viewed traditionally, historically, and contemporarily in this book. It seeks to confront the walls of hatred and remove the stones of oppression which hold people captive to brokenness, and calls them to the freedom where they can live as humble servants of Jesus Christ, the Lord. It notes that, in the community of believers, people can live together irrespective of their culture, class, race, gender, or place of birth. The servant model is profoundly needed in our world today, because it will help us to overcome our conflicts, competition, and domination of life.

Diplomatic dining, and political maneuvering, arising from cultural and gender biases, are exposed in a community sensitive to the presence of Christ. This approach to community building captures the spirit of transparency in our Lord's example when He took the towel of service to model how we may also overcome the "broken structures" (p. 12) in our disintegrating communities.

In effect, this book can become a breakpoint in the relational aspects of the church, or it can become a breakthrough, because it addresses the slaughtering of sacred cows, overturning of a false social order (p. 9), and a challenge for those who want to maintain the status quo of evil.

Today, in a fragmented world, there is a call for a new paradigm of "unity in diversity," and this is well echoed by Dr. Kennedy. We have in the church that which the world does not have to build this unity, and this study calls us to use this resource, i.e., to look to the center of life which is Jesus Christ. Relationships are frayed because we are not taking Christ seriously. In our effort to communicate with each other, we aren't talking *to*, but yelling *at* each other. Our challenge, then, is to take the words of Christ seriously - to wash one another's feet.

Academically speaking, Dr. Kennedy's scholarship is to be envied. He has demonstrated that a marginal ritual of the church might be retrieved and used to reconstruct community. We are very much encouraged to investigate practiced traditions and values which have been cast aside for generations and replaced by rituals of convenience and comfort. *The Politics of the Basin* recommends solution-oriented approaches and concepts to our difficulties with relationships, and seeks to teach the love that strengthens the church to make it more credible in an uncharitable age.

As President of the Seventh-day Adventist Church in the Atlantic Union, I personally want to thank Dr. Kennedy for his emphasis on a theme which has been so long neglected in the general Christian community. We can certainly speak about our similarities as Christians and learn many things from each other. In addition, we must continue to investigate the encompassing principles in John 13 so that we will be enabled to understand Christ's message for His church on how to build community as He would have it. Dr. Kennedy has made it clear that the divine goal for history is that all evil and meaninglessness will come to naught in the *finis* of the *eschaton*, when the community of believers shall sit with Christ in the eternal kingdom of our God.

Dr. David L. Taylor
South Lancaster
Massachusetts
June 1994

INTRODUCTION

The life of Christ has been the source from which I have drawn my inspiration for studying ecclesiology. However, a few moments in His life have been more potent for me than others. One such moment is the acted parable of the footwashing recorded in John 13. This parable was the catalyst for my doctoral dissertation, "The Search for Community," now more than a decade ago. I felt then, and still do feel, that the greatest lack in many churches is *community*. And I think the issue is most urgent especially at a time when socio-historical forces are telling us that hierarchy must give place to equality of participation, and relationships based on loving or "sacrificial service" rather than "power relationships." In effect, this book focuses on the church as community.

Chapter One, "The Politics of the Basin," uses footwashing to describe what the goal of community should be. It sets forth a brief history on the practice and traditions of footwashing in the Church and notes its contemporary cultural and spiritual understanding. It also notes how Jesus reinterpreted the act of footwashing, as a testimony of Christian faith and our comportment with each other.

Chapter Two embarks on a serious quest "to find community" and seeks to challenge those elements within the church which deprive it of community possibility. It notes that every community has a Judas in it who takes away from the unity which can be achieved. Judas can make a church just as dysfunctional as a normal family can be dysfunctional. The Judas person is a symbol of the power of destruction in the community.

In Chapter Three, the theme of power is developed further, and it is not denied that a coherent group needs a visible leader. That leader is not to be a "power" or "prestige broker," however, but a servant of Jesus Christ. In the footwashing framework, there is no room for manipulation or self-aggrandizement, so in the community of Christ where the Spirit leads, leaders and followers can know that sense of service which is based on sacrificial love.

Chapter Four focuses on the fact that the politics of the footwashing call for profound intimacy and mutuality. Such intimacy and mutuality have the goal of ushering in a new and solemn sense of fellowship with regard to community, for in the footwashing process, everyone - sooner or later - takes the servant's position and is forced to look up at the other instead of always looking down on the other. The point is to note the impact of humility which breaks down the natural barriers that exist between sinful humans so that all may be elevated to a higher plane of social awareness.

In Chapter Five, the question of servanthood is further developed, for it is seen as the community's public witness. It notes that willingness to follow Jesus is willingness to accept the Spirit's sending and to go even to the marginalized. And it also notes that our first choice or pleasure is simply to be in community together and avoid the aspects and issues of life that threaten us. In effect, the suggestion is that by bending down to wash dirty feet, we get a reflection of Jesus in the water which helps us overcome our own "rust" and superficiality so that we can truly build our church community.

In Chapter Six, we are confronted with the primary social unit - the blood family - for it is my feeling that one cannot speak of the church as community without confronting this aspect of life. Blood family is an important way for me to speak about ecclesiology since in metaphor the church is "The Household of God." And when a blood family is cohesive and whole, the church prospers. But if a blood family is disjunct and dysfunctional, the church suffers.

Chapter Seven notes that the only solution to broken lives and communities is forgiveness. "How can people love each other if they haven't forgiven each other?" is a question which must be faced again and again. Here are laid out steps for forgiveness in a community. It is natural to seek revenge. This is sinful nature. But to strive for forgiveness - imparted from above - is the only hope of community.

Chapter Eight develops the theme of holiness and community and calls for the understanding of love and justice which build community. It notes that in our effort to find community, we become separatists and forsake the ethical impact of holiness, thus losing the possibility of building loving and just Christian communities.

Chapter Nine notes that community building creates suffering, which began with the suffering of Christ. And it notes that the profound issue for the Christian is that while all people in this world suffer, the Christian suffers the most. But, that suffering in the Christian experience is different, since the Suffering Community shares in the suffering. A great significance in the suffering of Christians comes from the fact that they do not suffer alone.

Chapter Ten presents the idea that in footwashing we can find the meaning of all hope since it prepares us for the eschatological feast. The washing of each other's feet reminds us of the gathering of God's people at the fellowship of the Feast of Love.

This emphasis on community hardly makes it necessary for me to state that this book has been a community project. Its communal dimensions are too obvious from the number of scholars, colleagues, and other persons to whom I refer in each aspect of the theme. I must identify, however, the particular influences of Professor William Bean Kennedy, my advisor at Union Theological Seminary in New York. He had to do with my first foolish attempt to make of John 13 a large study. And seconding him is my friend, present colleague, and team teacher in Philosophy of Religion, Dr. Norman Wendth, who has been for me the greatest contributor to the richness of my discussion. He was not afraid to be my first frank critic. Other colleagues such as Dr. Lee Parson, Dr. Ann Parrish, and former colleague Jeanette Bryson have been valuable contributors, by being sounding boards. My worthy students, especially Heidi Ward, Talbert Knight, and George Sekasen, who read and shared their understanding of the full draft, have certainly helped me with perspective. And thanks to Ellen Fisk-Biek for being patient with my drafts upon drafts. She knows more than any other person how writing on community can make one do mind changes.

Greatest thanks, however, to my most intimate biological and spiritual community: To June, my wife, a mother and a teacher, and our three sons - Robert, Leighton and Sheldon, because they have likely been frustrated but faithful in listening to me when I wanted to bounce off an idea and when I prayed around them for community.

But none of the above can take responsibilities for my ideas, my errors and my miscalculations. They were mine and remain mine -- for while I stand in community -- my sins are mine.

THE POLITICS OF THE BASIN:
A Perspective on the Church as Community

The Politics of the Basin

The ritual of footwashing, which I shall call "the politics of the basin," is not just something that is done every day; it is something that can be done in a special way. Just before Maundy Thursday (Holy Thursday), the pastor of a Protestant congregation in Amesbury was searching for a worship service that would create community in his church. After speaking to a few friends, he came up with an idea. Though he was nervous about suggesting it to his worship committee, he resisted his negative feelings and went ahead to suggest footwashing prior to the Eucharist for his total congregation. With a little discussion the committee bought the idea, and nearly forty members of the congregation attended the footwashing ceremony. Then came an evaluation from the chair-person of the committee: "a feeling of joy and love all wrapped up in one, a feeling of warmth for other persons, although some of the people I barely knew, a feeling of concern for those persons flowed from me to them and back as a special togetherness, a secret bond of caring." From the pastor's point of view, the congregation was better prepared to

understand the sacraments than they had ever been before. A
feeling of quiet joy seemed to bubble up and out of everyone;
hugs were abundant, enthusiasm was boundless, and all felt
that God's Spirit had moved among them (Kent Richmond, "A
Secret Bond of Caring," *The Christian Ministry*, Jan. '79, pp.
9-10).

In Amesbury, the footwashing was novel, and enthusiasm
and novelty may have created a response because the
footwashing was being practiced for the first time. But there
are those for whom footwashing is a ritual, and they speak of
the potent, creative, emotive experiencing of their symbolic
relationship as "warm," "intimate," "cheerful," "celebrative,"
"meditative," and "hopeful." In my own experience I have
participated in many footwashing celebrations in Seventh-day
Adventist churches. During such celebrations, I have noted a
profound transforming atmosphere of worship and a strong
sense of community. Some people are involved in singing,
some are washing feet, others are talking, while others are
praying. While the central issue is footwashing, people engage
in it in different ways, still sensing their involvement,
participation, and belonging.

It is during these times of community building that people
become vulnerable and willing to be reconciled to one another.
One might debate today how much concerted effort is put into
the building of community, but I can recall how we as children
watched with eager anticipation as those who harbored
resentments sought to cast aside their differences and were
reconciled. There was always a special moment when people
would embrace and repeat the words, "If we never get to do
this again, let us do it on the other side." Today, it seems that
much of the older tradition has been shifting, and such aspects
as public confession and repentance are not so emphasized.
Yet in many places footwashing is still seen as an occasion to
"tell the truth" about the community's relationships, make
confessions about any brokenness, and seek to remove barriers
which have been created over time. Participants are even
invited to stand in a circle holding hands, while a designated

leader from the circle speaks of those missing, particularly those who have died since the last celebration. A final challenge for faithfulness calls everyone to join in singing a song of hope such as, "Will the Circle Be Unbroken Bye and Bye" or a song of fellowship such as, "Blest Be the Tie That Binds."

Thus, the Seventh-day Adventist Church is one of the few Christian churches that retain the practice of footwashing as a rite of worship. In its 1986 _Church Manual_, it is noted that at the celebration of the Communion Service, the congregation should participate in the Ordinance of Humility (Footwashing). The deacons and deaconesses provide towels, basins, buckets, and hot or cold water, for the washing of feet. Also, those officiating ensure that no one is left out (p. 79). In its 1992 _Minister's Manual_, it is emphasized that footwashing is a powerful symbol which carries a profound personal impact and leads people to confront themselves and provides a lesson in humility (p. 214).

The assumption is that the foundation for the practice of footwashing is in the order which was laid down by Christ, as He shared in the Last Supper with His disciples in the Upper Room (John 13). Just to remind us, here is a brief summary of the introductory note to the story:

> Jesus knowing that the Father had given all things into his hands and that he had come from God and was going to God, rose from supper, laid aside his garments and girded himself with a towel. Then he poured water into a basin and began to wash his disciples' feet, and to wipe them with the towel with which he was girded (John 13:3-5 NRSV).

In early Adventist history, the celebration of footwashing was accepted as a command. And one hears in the words of one of Adventism's earliest pioneers:

When Jesus Christ was here below
He taught His people what to do;
And if we would His precepts keep,
We must attend to washing feet.

For on that night He was betrayed,
He for us all a pattern laid-
Soon as His supper He did eat,
He rose and washed His brethren's feet.

The Lord who made the earth and sky,
Arose and laid His garments by;
And washed their feet to show that we,
Like Christ, should always humble be.

He washed them all, that all were clean,
Save Judas who was full of sin.
May none of us, like Judas sell
Our Lord for gold and go to hell.

Said Peter, Lord, it shall not be;
Thou shalt not stoop to washing me:
Oh! that no Christian now may say,
I cannot Jesus' word obey.

Ye call Me Lord and Master, too;
Then do as I have done to you;
All my commands and sayings keep,
And show your love by washing feet.

Ye shall be happy, if ye know
And do these things, by faith below;
For I'll protect you till I come,
And then I'll take you to your home.

The Lord of glory stoops to men,
And an example sets for them:
If in humility complete,
Salute the saints and wash their feet.

(From James White, *Hymns for God's Peculiar People*, 1849).

Footwashing is Deeply Rooted in Christian Tradition.

Although footwashing is not generally being practiced in mainline churches today, it has had a long historical tradition in the Christian Church. Following the practice from Judaism, the earliest church accepted it along with the Passover. And it is significant to consider how Christ interpreted it by noting that anyone who refused it could not have a share in His kingdom (Jn. 13:8). This higher concern is what attracts me most, and I shall propose it as the major point which Christ sought to teach through footwashing to His disciples.

Not much is said of footwashing in Apostolic history, except for the fact that Mary had washed the feet of Jesus (Lk. 7:36-50; Jn. 12: 1-8) and Paul's one cryptic reference that those who would be accounted as true widows in the community must "wash the saints' feet" (1 Tim. 5:10). For a while, in the post-apostolic age, footwashing was understood to be mandatory. Thus, Augustine cited it in his Epistle to Januarium while Bernard recommended it in _De Caena Domini_ as "a daily sacrament for the remission of sins." In the Greek Church it was also regarded as a "mystery." Paul Tschachert, whose historical sketch I am following, argues that nowhere does he find testimony that footwashing became a general, public, solemn ecclesiastical act in early Christian history. He explains, however, that the ceremony was and still is solemnly performed in certain places where a number of bishops and monastic superiors wash the feet of twelve persons who are invited for the occasion on an annual basis. The subjects are usually twelve poor old men or twelve priests.

Tschachert also notes that the reformers, especially Luther (cf. his Maundy Thursday sermon concerning footwashing in the _Hauspostille_), opposed "that hypocritical footwashing, in which one stoops to wash the feet of his inferior, but expects still more humility in return." Upon this basis the Reformed Church has endeavored only to impress the meaning of Christ's act on the hearts of individuals by diligently proclaiming His

Gospel. At Schwabisch Hall in Wurttemberg on the Wednesday before Easter every year, a special *Fusswaschungspredigt* is still delivered in St. Catherine's Church. While in the Lutheran Church footwashing has been considered as "an abominable papal corruption," there are occasions on which it is still practiced. In the year 1817, the Upper Consistory at Dresden condemned twelve Lutheran citizens of Weida to public penance for having permitted Duke Maurice William (at that time still a Roman Catholic) to wash their feet.

The Church of England at first carried out the letter of the command to wash feet. The ceremony was originally performed by the reigning sovereign. The sovereign would wash the feet of thirteen subjects on Maundy Thursday. The subjects were usually drawn from among the poor. But as time passed, the sovereign began to designate the Minister of State to do the washing, and so the practice lost its significance and fell into disuse. Of course, the practice persists in a few Church of England churches and is still being used on Maundy Thursday, mainly by the officers of the Church to encourage fellowship.

Many minor Baptist groups also observe the custom. The Ana-baptists declared in favor of footwashing, appealing to John 13:14 and also to 1 Timothy 5:10. They considered it as a sacrament instituted by Christ Himself, "Whereby our being washed by the blood of Christ and his example of deep humiliation is to be impressed upon us" (Confession of United Baptists and Mennonites, 1660).

The Moravians revived the footwashing with their love feasts. However, they did not strictly enforce it or confine it to Maundy Thursday. It was performed not only by the leaders toward their followers, but also by the latter among themselves, during the singing of a hymn explanatory of the symbol. This practice was finally abolished by the Moravian Synod in 1818 (see Paul Tschachert, "Foot-washing," *New Schaff Herzog Encyclopedia,* Vol. VI, pp. 339-340).

G. H. Frank Knight adds to Paul Tschachert's historical account by stating that footwashing was a practice rooted in the early history of Judaism and in all Middle Eastern cultures. In such cultures, he notes that footwashing had two major purposes:

(a) Ceremonial cleansing before worship; and
(b) As an act of hospitality to welcome guests to a home.

In Judah, much defilement was attached to the feet which were imperfectly protected from the dirt of their dusty highways, thus, ceremonial washing was required before any of the priests could worthily approach the place of sacrifice (Ex. 30:18-21; 40:30-32, cf; 2 Chr. 4:6). As such, many brazen vessels were placed between the Tabernacle and the Altar of Burnt Offering, and much washing of feet and washing of hands was carried out. According to Tosefta Men.i., it was the practice of the priests to wash their hands and feet twice in the basin to ensure a proper cleansing. On Sabbaths and on the Day of Atonement, as well as on 9th Ab, the custom was not so rigorously followed, except in the case of one arriving from a journey. But that does not mean that the ceremonial law of footwashing was not rigorously followed.

The history of Christian worship of the second century and later reveals that churches were provided with an atrium in the area of the court surrounded with porticoes or cloisters. Standing in the middle of the atrium was a fountain called Cantharis, or Philala, where the worshippers washed their feet and hands before entering the Church. Eusebius says, in his panegyric regarding the Church, that "On entering within the gates, you are not permitted to enter immediately, with impure and unwashed feet" (*HE x 4*). It is noted that, in a temple erected by Panlinus, an extensive space was left between the temple and the vestibule which was decorated and enclosed with four inclined porticoes. In the space were placed the symbols of the sacred purifications which afforded the means of cleansing to those who proceeded to the inner parts of the sanctuary.

In ancient Coptic worship, as noted in the *Canons of Christodulus* (11th cent.), worshippers were required to come barefoot to worship. A tank was therefore placed in the floor in order to afford facilities for worshippers to cleanse their feet and wipe off the dust of travel before entering into their sacred devotions. The present-day use of shoes in modern Coptic churches has rendered the strict observance of this practice no longer necessary.

By way of support for this survey, I note Frank Knight's argument for a long history of footwashing. First, he cites the Early Old Testament, where footwashing is found, when Abraham and Lot carried out "the hospitable act" for their guests (Gen. 18:4; 19:2). Then he turns to New Testament times where Jesus reproaches Simon for his neglect of providing for the act. Then Jesus considers the loving action of Mary a message of the Gospel to be mentioned to the world (Lk. 7:36-50).

In his conclusion, Knight says that John 13 is the central statement on footwashing and the *Locus Classicus* for hospitality found in Biblical and Christian history. He admits that there are deeper meanings, but he argues that the emphasis on the custom of hospitality is dominant. In this case, he feels other issues must remain in the background (G. Frank Knight, "Feetwashing," *Encyclopedia of Religion and Ethics*, pp. 814, 915). As we shall see from its historical context, hospitality was quite significant as an interpretation of footwashing. Ailand J. Hultgreen has given this focus in his summary of footwashing from apostolic times to contemporary times. According to his summary, two major streams of interpretations have developed: (1) One notes that the footwashing is to be seen exclusively as an example of humility given by Jesus for others, and therefore it has no sacramental or soteriological significance. (2) The other argues that the footwashing of John 13 has further meanings while still embracing the first. But the dominant issue is hospitality.

Other issues such as the purification of believers (through baptism, the word of Jesus, or believing Jesus); the sacramental meaning (baptism, eucharist, penance, or even the footwashing itself as a sacrament); the soteriological meaning, signifying Jesus' submission to death on the cross; the act having topological background in the Old Testament; and an account which functions as an etiology for the practice of footwashing in the Johannine Church are evident. But Hultgreen suggests that the largest issue is hospitality. For Hultgreen, John 13 has gone through various editorships, and, therefore, one cannot be sure with what seriousness to take footwashing much more than as a hospitable act. Thus, footwashing as a rite, concludes Hultgreen, need not be celebrated by the Christian Church today (_New Testament Studies_, Vol. 28, pp. 539-546).

As one reads a scholar such as C. K. Barrett, one is fascinated by his keen insight, for he argues that in the whole Passion Story, John 13 stands first as "a symbolic narrative," and prefigures the crucifixion itself, and the way to the re-interpretation of the crucifixion. The crucifixion as the public act of Jesus on Calvary explicitly spelled out His private act in the presence of the disciples. Each act is a narrative of humility and service that proceeds from the love of Jesus for His own. The cleansing of the disciples' feet represents their own cleansing from sin by the sacrificial blood of Christ (Jn. 1:29; 19:34). When the significance of what is taking place is caught by Peter, he exclaims, "Lord, not my feet only, but also my head and my hands" (Jn. 13:9). So Jesus being lifted up on the cross draws all of humankind to himself (Jn. 12:32).

A further aspect of Barrett's exposition states that just as the cross is the temporal manifestation of the eternal movement of Christ from the Father, so the footwashing is enacted by Jesus in full recognition of the incarnation (Jn. 13:1,3). Here Barrett suggests that perhaps, in a secondary way, baptism and the eucharist are also prefigured, for the act of washing is what the story of salvation is all about. As such, footwashing is a divine deed by which the believer may symbolize release from sin.

Out of the two-fold significance of the footwashing Barrett argues that through the work of Christ, God has cleansed a people for Himself. The people are not all cleansed, for Satan finds in Judas, one of the twelve, a tool ready to be used. The apostles, the disciples, and the servants of Jesus must recognize this treachery. They must show in their lives the humility of Jesus. They must take up the cross and follow Jesus. So instead of being traitors they may share Jesus' authority. Those who represent the Church are the responsible envoys of Christ. And they share His dignity and are obliged to copy His humility and service. Notwithstanding its authority, the Church enjoys no absolute security, since even one of the twelve may prove to be a traitor. At the end, Judas will go out into the darkness, and Jesus will be alone with the faithful. In the original story, the disciples are slow of heart, and their loyalty is about to be shaken to the foundations, but to them the mystery will be unfolded (C.K. Barrett, *The Gospel According to St. John*, pp. 363-364).

From a social perspective, Scott Peck comments on Beatrice Bruteau's series of lectures, "The Holy Thursday Revolution," given in 1991 at Wilson College, Pennsylvania, in which she notes that the greatest revolution in the history of humankind occurred on Maundy Thursday -- the day before Jesus' crucifixion. The revolution took place in two stages. The first stage occurred when Jesus washed the feet of His disciples. Up until that moment, the whole point of things had been for someone to get to the top or else attempt to get further up. But the revolution began when the man already on the top -- a rabbi, a teacher, a master -- lowered Himself and began to wash the disciples' feet. In one moment, Jesus symbolically overturned the whole social order. Hardly comprehending what was happening, even His own disciples were horrified by His behavior. The second stage of the revolution concerned the establishing of the Last Supper in the symbolic form of communion. These two revolutions brought to the Early Church the dynamic nature of community (*The Different Drum*, p. 294).

Community a Potent Interpretation of Footwashing

Donald Kraybill also argues concerning the revolutionary nature of the footwashing when he says that the cross as a Roman symbol was a harsh sign of the state power to execute criminals, while footwashing, which was not so politicized, was Jesus' choice as the sign of the Kingdom (_The Upside Down Kingdom_). Indeed, a very radical observation, but quite interesting and one that needs further attention in light of the fact that there is a tendency among Christians to use the cross as the sign of political power and a key to domination. In a word, footwashing should help us to correct dominating tendencies, since as the dramatic parable of the kingdom, it leads us to the Cross of Christ, not as a sign of power but as a sign of humble, self-sacrificing love. It helps us to focus on the reality of our lives as servants of Christ. The Cross as the footwashing is a parable that tells us that we are called to repentance, and not to exaltation. We are called not to the cultivation of the individualistic spirit, but to develop the spirit of love and humility.

According to Ellen White, just before Christ received His baptism of suffering, He wanted His disciples to understand the spirit of love and humility. Therefore He used the noble illustration of footwashing to impress this upon their minds forever. As the disciples sat together with Him in the Upper Room nursing their secret feelings about who would be the greatest, He read their hearts, and then demonstrated what it meant to be their Lord and Servant (_Desire of Ages_, pp. 642-651). In the following words, she says it well:

> The ordinance of humility most forcibly illustrates the necessity of true ministry. This ordinance was to be observed by the disciples, that they might ever keep in mind the lessons of humility and ministry that Christ had given them. Not long before this, John and James had come to their Master with the request, "We would that Thou shouldest do for us whatsoever

we shall desire. And He said to them, What would
ye that I should do for you? They said unto Him,
Grant unto us that we may sit, one on Thy right
hand, and the other on Thy left, in Thy glory." The
other disciples were very displeased by the request.
Jesus called them all to Him, and talked with them
about it: "Ye know that they which are accounted for
to rule over the Gentiles exercise lordship over them;
and their great ones exercise authority upon them.
But so shall it not be among you; but whosoever will
be great among you, shall be your minister; and
whosoever of you will be the chiefest, shall be
servant of all. For even the Son of man came not to
be ministered unto, but to minister, and give His life
a ransom for many ("Ministry," *Signs of the Times*,
1900).

Sharing in an Ignored Ritual

All of the data and interpretations presented thus far are
intended to make the point that when we practice the ritual of
footwashing, we do so with the assurance that we are sharing
in an ignored ritual that draws us into the memorable history
of Jesus Christ. In his book, *The Magic of Rituals*, Tom
Driver has pointed out that rituals are hated by some
Christians. And yet, rituals have much to do with our lives.
While rituals might be the means by which we are oppressed
and by which we oppress others, yet, without rituals, we dare
not find our "way" into the freedoms of the future. Rituals
function as pathways through which we create order for our
lives, communicate with others, and create social change. In
effect, rituals are a vital way of going from the inchoate to the
expressive, from instability to harmony, thus they help us to
find order, community, and transforming directions for our
lives.

My extended discussion will explain how as a sign of the kingdom the act of footwashing as a spiritual ritual might lead to the most profound experiencing of community intended for the Church. The water of footwashing has played a decisive role in the life of humanity, in the Church, and in life generally. For Mircea Eliade, water reminds us of our interconnectedness and the capacity of such linkage to carry grace and destruction (_The Sacred and the Profane, The Nature of Religion_, pp. 127-132). The use of water in the Church acknowledges its acceptance of the life-giving power of Christ -- His cleansing, reconciling, and healing impact. It also acknowledges the presence of the Holy Spirit who as breath (wind) and power is the creative force in awakening people to Christian life, then sealing them in baptism for fellowship within the community of faith. In effect, the water of the Spirit brings Christ close so that a person can reflect on the humble suffering Christ who is exalted as Lord and Savior of life. As A. M. Toplady (1740-1778) said in that well-known hymn, "Let the water and the blood, from the riven side which flowed, be of sin the double cure; cleanse me from its guilt and power" ("Rock of Ages").

Tom Driver's discussion of rituals rightly refers to Juan Segundo's view of footwashing as the "God-present experience" in which the Spirit draws us near and presses us together as believers (_The Magic of Rituals_, p. 208). As the sign of grace, hope, and faith, footwashing proclaims the faithfulness of Jesus. For Jurgen Moltmann, baptism is "the unique sign of grace" while the Lord's Supper is "the repeatable sign of hope." Both are linked to one another in the Messianic Community (_The Church in the Power of the Spirit_, p. 243). What Moltmann has not told is how they are linked. I propose that they are linked through the potent "ritual of faith." I say this because it takes living faith (_Pistes_ and _Pisteuo_) to build community. Letty Russell, who has written much on community, says that faith, like partnership, is a relationship of trust with God and others that is given to us. "Faith is caught not taught" (see "Good Housekeeping" in

Feminist Theology: A Reader, pp. 230-231). Ronald Marstin
agrees with Russell's understanding when he says that faith
gathers us together and keeps us in the community through
grace and hope. That is, our faith expressed in footwashing
helps us to break open life's structures of exclusion, and widen
the opportunity for people to realize that they matter, that they
can be happy as children of God. All those committed to the
worship of the just God, says Marstin, must come to the
recognition that God stands above the partisan loyalties of the
tribal gods. They must understand that in God, there is neither
Jew nor Greek, male nor female, for all are equal in Christ
(Gal. 3:25). Through such faith they must learn to trust each
other and commit themselves to each other. For while they
celebrate community life, they must still be conscious of the
broken structures in which they live and pray that God will
help them overcome the broken structures (cf. Ronald Marstin,
Beyond Tribal Gods; The Maturing of Faith, pp. 88-89).

For Karl Barth, faith is from first to last the work of the
Holy Spirit. And the church exists only as it stands on the
reality of this faith and this Spirit. Since we come to know the
gift of faith by the Holy Spirit, our lives already have an
eschatological existence with the Lord, but we are not yet with
Him in the ultimate consumation. Faith has a present and a
future dimension. In its present, we see its reality most
transparently in the life of the believing community, while we
see its future dimension as a promise which finds its reality
in the *parousia* and the future vestal community (*Church
Dogmatics*, IV:3, p. 740).

The reality of faith makes me argue against life's
brokenness as it is today. We live in a time when community
within the Church has just about disintegrated. Where
community does exist, it is conceived as individualistic,
privatistic, vertical or horizontal, and humanistic. As a
consequence, people are trying to use all kinds of trivial
means to solidify their relationships, but are finding no
situation where they enjoy a reconciled life with God and their
fellow humanity.

In taking this challenge seriously, I propose that the ritual of footwashing can call us back to the Church's roots: to the _radis_ - the Upper Room - where Spiritual community (_koinonia_), the community of faith, hope and love, found its very beginning. From the Upper Room of the footwashing we move to the human community, for as Rudolf Bultmann correctly said, people's individual lives are not annihilated (lost in a mystical or vertical bond) by their relationship to God, but, on the contrary, they are awakened to their own reality in the presence of others (_Jesus and the Word_, pp. 153-154).

To love God, as we shall be insisting throughout, means to love our neighbors, fellow-members, and enemies as well. "The politics of the basin" (footwashing) is a critical tool to help us determine in practical ways the meaning of our commitments to love. Footwashing commands us, as it were, to break away from our isolation, loneliness, brokenness, and self-seeking, to live in truth, and in love. It unmasks us and calls us to obedience, for, either we can reject it and our Lord, or we can receive it and submit to the authority of the One who stands above the community in its awakening, through the Latter's upbuilding and its mission. This understanding resonates Karl Barth, but it is my conviction that no ritual of the church can build community effectively until it is practiced with a critical orientation to Christ.

CHRIST THE LORD

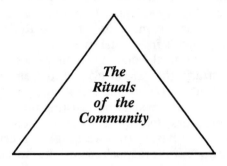

The
Rituals
of the
Community

The Church as Community

The Church has one foundation,
'Tis Jesus Christ the Lord;
She is His new creation,
By water and the word;
From heaven He came and sought her
To be His holy bride;
With His own blood He bought her,
And for her life He died.
(Samuel Stone, 1866).

CHAPTER TWO

CHALLENGE TO UNITY:
Power and Influence in the Community

Judas, the Cause for Community Brokenness

The idea of a Judas sitting at the supper table (Jn. 13:2) has angered many people. They want to know why such an enemy was there in spite of Christ's knowledge that he had already betrayed Jesus. However, his presence has more to say about the reality of community life -- even in the churches -- than if he were absent. Based upon his reading of Luke 9:46, which states "there arose a reasoning among the disciples which of them should be the greatest," Dietrich Bonhoeffer has this to say:

We know who it is that sows this thought in the Christian community. But perhaps we do not bear in mind enough that no Christian community ever comes together without this thought ever emerging as a seed of discord. Thus at the very beginning of Christian fellowship there is engendered   an invisible, often unconscious, life and death contest. "There arose a reasoning among them." This is enough to destroy a fellowship. Hence it is

virtually necessary that every Christian community,
from the very outset, face this dangerous enemy
squarely, and eradicate it (*Life Together*, p. 90).

That is, in the development of Christian community, there
is always a Judas (both a traitor and critic of the true disciples
and servants of Jesus), and there are always those whose
superficiality provides opportunity to break every form of
harmony.   Pride, prejudice, and lust for power are only some
of the means by which community has been broken.   When
Bonhoeffer says that "Community is not simply to be taken for
granted," he means that in the struggle to find community,
these forces of evil are always present to create conflict. Ellen
G. White comments that, "Till the close of time there will be
a conflict between the church of God and those who are under
the control of evil angels" (*Acts of the Apostles*, p. 219).
Concentration on the self, self-centeredness, and selfish
ambition always lead to the elimination of others from one's
society.   So as we seek to focus on ecclesiology, we must
exorcise any oppressive and dominating element which destroys
community.
   I have seen a lot of broken churches and sometimes
dislike discussing them, for the images are too painful for me.
But what Scott Peck says is precisely how I can describe my
own experience of the brokenness I have seen.

On my lecture tours across the country the one
constant I have found wherever I go - the
Northeast, Southeast, Midwest, Southwest, or West
Coast - is the lack of - and the thirst for -
community.   This lack and thirst is particularly
heartbreaking in those places where one might
expect to find real community: in churches.
Speaking to my audiences, I often say, "Please

don't ask me questions during the break times. I need those times to get my thoughts together. Besides, it has invariably been my experience that the questions you have represent concerns that others have as well and that they are best addressed in the group as a whole." But more often than not someone will come to me during the break with a question. When I say, "I thought I requested you not to," the usual response is "Yes, but, Dr. Peck, this is terribly important to me, and I can't ask it in the group because some of the members of my church are here." I wish I could say this was an exception. There are, of course, exceptions and exceptional churches. But such a remark speaks of the normal level of trust and intimacy and vulnerability in our churches and other so-called 'communities' (*The Different Drum*, p. 57).

The feeling that no one can be trusted, the sense that people are lost, the focus on "the survival of the fittest" are realities of life that can be seen everywhere in contemporary culture. Life for many people, aptly described, is competition and self-assertiveness, both of which disregard all attempts to find community. In their reflection on Alexis de Tocqueville's idea of community, Robert Bellah and his colleagues have lamented the brokenness of the West in *Habits of the Heart*, by noting that instead of a citizenry of cooperators, all we can find is a citizenship of individual competitors, with each person attending to his/her own interest and each seeking to find his/her own success. In this competitiveness, success is sought at all cost, even at the sacrifice of all communities - marriages, families, churches and even the nation. The strongest reality in people's lives is not community, but the egotistic self. Therefore, mutual trust and sacrificial love are superfluous.

John 13: A Challenge to Things Which Destroy Community

I submit, therefore, that the significance of John 13 is that it presents us with a radical challenge to the self-interest and to all the barriers which are often built to destroy community today. When one reads the drama, one is not so aware at first of the underlying contention among the disciples. John does not allude to it. He only points to the fact that among the disciples there was a traitor. "Satan," he says, "had entered into Judas Iscariot" (v.2). That might seem minimal, but a more penetrating look shows that Judas alone was sufficient for community disruption. In the Judas type, there was radical individual self-interest and the seed was sown among all of the disciples (Lk. 22:24).

Instead of a feast at the Lord's table in joyful community, what was present was "Diplomatic Dining." The fishermen found it hard to be with the tax collector, while the "Sons of Thunder" found it hard to be with the zealot (cf. F. F. Bruce, *New Testament History*, p. 183). Each one wanted to exercise a certain strategic plan to reach a position of power and gain social prestige. The only concern for each of them was "the place of honor." The problem, as we shall focus on it, is that each sought to manipulate and oppress the other in their striving to reach the top. Since they knew that only Jesus could really be at the top, they were simply struggling not to be at the bottom (cf. Richard Foster, "The Ministry of the Towel: Practicing Love through Service," (*Christianity Today*, Jan. 7, 1983, pp. 18-21). When the disciples entered the Upper Room, their hearts were full of resentful feelings. Judas pressed next to Christ on the left side; John was on the right. And if there were a higher place, in choosing his position at the table, Judas would have tried to place himself closer. Christ, the True Servant, served Judas first (Ellen G. White,

Desire of Ages, p. 645).

A colleague of mine described his interpretation of the disciples' juggling of relationships and the trade-off to reach the top in this way:

> If you work out the secret calculations of each disciple in American government equivalent, it could be said that Judas wished to be Secretary of the Treasury; Peter, President or Minister of State; John and James, Vice Presidents; and Andrew, Ambassador-at-Large. All had conceived of a position of power as they perceived it in a temporal kingdom. They judged themselves and thought themselves well fitted for a place of honor.

Challenging Structures of Power

In his book, _Beyond Tragedy_, Reinhold Niebuhr describes the politics of power and its impact on community by stating that those who seek power are necessary to the kingdoms of the world. They organize society. They build up empires. They build civilizations. But they do all of this with physical force. Only in this way can they achieve a type of unstable unity. In effect, they are pretentious individualists who serve society only if it will get them to the top of the social order. But in doing so, their pride is exposed in their contempt for other people (pp.197-207).

The political philosopher Mikhail Bakunin notes in a similar vein that there are persons in our world who seem to have no personal interests, no affairs, no sentiments, no attachments, no property, not even a name of their own. Everything about them is absorbed by one exclusive interest, one thought, one passion - "the revolution." Though they seem

totally altruistic as they go about with talk of justice and
fairness, yet they show every strain of evil by their lust for
power.   Instead of genuine love and the search for the
corporate life, what they really exhibit is manipulative force
that seeks to get them to the top of the order (cf., *A Political
Philosophy of Bakunin*).

For novelist John Braine, the pretense of these
individualists soon shows.   For the introduction of his little
book, *Room at the Top*, Braine says:

> This little book is about the violence which a young
> man does to himself and to others in his struggle to
> rise above the world of his childhood.   Joe
> Llampton, whose story it is, was brought up on the
> fringes of poverty and squalor in an ugly north
> country town, and has emerged with one over-
> riding aim: to fight his way up into the bright world
> of money and influence.
>
> When he comes to a new town and a new job and
> starts to live among comfortably well off, intelligent
> people, it looks as if the campaign is succeeding.
> Since he is an attractive and energetic young man,
> it is not long before a very pretty girl with a rich
> father falls in love with him.
>
> Only one thing holds him back: he is himself in
> love with another woman.   She is older than he, her
> looks are beginning to fade, and she is married
> already.   But between them an extraordinary love
> grows up, a passion of both the heart and the
> senses, in which each of them find a fulfillment
> deeper than they had ever dreamed possible.   In an
> idyll of four summer days their love reaches its

culmination and its end because here Joe Llampton's demon for success takes over and brings about the book's tragic, ironic end.

Today, historians are still debating the real causes for World War I.   Some argue that imperialism, militarism, nationalism, and the lack of an international forum for the resolution of the underlying problems were among the major concerns. It can be said, however, that whatever the causes were, our world still mourns the death of more than 8.5 million soldiers killed in the war, 21 million wounded while 8 million were taken as prisoners. World War II lacked logical causes even more. The social interpretation was that Germany was not satisfied about the Treaty of Versailles and wanted revenge by becoming the _only_ international power. The psychological interpretation was that Hitler was a totally "crazy man" who wanted to create a _super race._ He was influential enough to get a large group of people having their own self-interests to act with him. The stain on history we remember the most is the holocaust, which took the lives of six million Jews and an estimate of that many Christians, as well. The real causes of these wars are still said to be anybody's guess. But while historians continue to argue their real causes, we can lay the discussion to rest by paraphrasing T. S. Eliot's words, that half of the harm that is done in this world is due to people who want to feel important. They don't mean to do harm, but the harm does not interest them, or they do not see it, or they justify it because they are absorbed in the endless struggle to think well of themselves (noted in J. Hamilton, _Serendipity_, p. 69). Their lust for power, their misuse of power and their abuse of power have led them to despise people and destroy community.   In the unspiritual structures of the world, where people are regarded as having the right to exercise control over the lives of others by virtue of the positions they hold within their social structure, power is violent and destructive. Sad to say, often in the church this same violence and destruction abide. In many churches, the violence is often masked in "piety" or in the myth of some "divine election." As such we should decry the motley mix of the struggle for power which goes on at church "election times" (cf. Basil Moore (ed.), *The Challenge of Black Theology in South Africa*). J. S. Hamilton has rightly said about the abuse of power that the sin is not only in the hunger for the top, but in the shabby, pathetic ways in which those who seek it treat others (*Serendipity*, p.78). In effect, as we seek community in our churches, we must exorcise the spirits of power which cause us to be so power-hungry and competitive that we destroy each other.

Three Basic Principles for Reshaping Community

The footwashing tells us to arise from the table, upturn our view of life and focus on those principles that can organize, constitute, and guarantee community. The earthly historical reality of the church says it also lives where the mixture of confidence and suspicion has destroyed the fabric of its spiritual harmony. While I shall take many things into account in a longer study, here, I suggest three basic principles which move us from life in a humanistic view, and life in a privatistic view, to life in a spiritual sense. The principles are:

1.   The Need for Humility

The first principle that challenges the abuse of power is humility. I place this first because the greatest characteristics of Jesus' life were humble obedience and self-renunciation

(William Barclay, _The Letters to the Philippians, Colossians and Thessalonians_, p. 38). This is how the Scriptures show it, "He humbled Himself and became obedient to the point of death, even death on a cross" (Phil. 2:5-8). Humility, which has been associated with several biblical words, suggests ideas such as love, gentleness, consideration, meekness, forbearance, patience, graciousness, and kindness. And it is a misappropriation when it is connected with humiliation, servitude, weakness or false piety, and penance, as some persons would seek to represent. Rather, humility arises from noblemindedness, wisdom, and Godliness that comes about when people are linked to Christ and conformed to His image (cf., W. Bender and H. H. Esser, articles on "Humility" in _The New International Dictionary of New Testament Theology_, Colin Brown, gen. ed., pp. 256-264). In bending down to wash the disciples' feet, Jesus attacked their self-importance, boastfulness, rudeness, pride, anxiousness to impress, and all the efforts at celebrity or self-upliftment so that they could focus on the Christ-like character. Christ showed that the way _up_ was _down_. He showed that the "Halls of Fame" and the "Who's Who" are not necessary for the kingdom, thus calling every disciple to let **Him** be the _center_ and the _circumference_ of their lives.

Defined further, humility refers to the way people see themselves before God and how they describe their response to the awareness that they live under the cross of Christ. The cross is the place where the one who recognizes his/her failure finds a sober assessment of his/her status in relationship to God and other people. It offers a place for the confession of our equality and commonality before God and a place where we can right our failure or repent (_metanoia_) of our mistreatment of others. According to Roger Crook, the person who is humble before God cannot be arrogant with other persons. The humble person does not seek preferential treatment, does not impose upon other people, does not presume an unwarranted status, nor does he/she make claims about personal achievements or personal abilities. Therefore, he recognizes with Jesus that the greatest in the kingdom will be "like a little child" (*An Introduction to Christian Ethics*, p.73; Matt. 18:1-3). This simple definition of humility means that self is put in the background and Christ and others are in the foreground. Now, there is a false form of humility which is used for manipulation. Jesus identified it in the Pharisees when He spoke of the two worshippers in the temple. He also commented on it when He spoke of the kind of fasting and prayer done by those who sought special favors of God and the respect of the people. Paul also pointed to it when, speaking to a divided church in Corinth, he said:

> Consider your own call brothers and sisters: not many of you were wise by human standards, not many were powerful, not many were of noble birth. But God chose what is foolish in the world to shame the wise; God chose what is weak in the world to shame the foolish; God chose what is low and despised in the world, things that are not, to reduce to nothing the things that are, so that no one might boast in the presence of God (1 Cor. 1:26-28).

In effect, the humility which the church is called to practice is the humility of Jesus, the type of humility patterned after the incarnation of Jesus (Phil. 2:5-8). That is, the "self emptying" and acceptance of the love of humanity as it is known in Jesus. Lionel Thornton believes that as soon as we begin to ask wherein the fellowship of the church consists, we must turn to its relationship *in* and *through* Jesus Christ. In His life we share in the church, for the church is not primarily that of a human fellowship, but its distinctive character is manifested in fellowship with its divine source (*The Common Life in the Body of Christ*, pp. 47,327 quoted in J. R. Nelson, *Criterion for the Church*, pp. 51-52). Karl Barth develops this idea effectively when he notes that Christ guarantees the first dimension (or visible existence) of the church, and the second dimension (the invisible existence), through His sacrifice on the cross. He is its third dimension as the Lamb of God (see, *Church Dogmatics*, IV:1, "The Being of the Community"). If this is understood properly enough, it will lessen our problems with pride, prejudice, prejudgment, racism, sexism, ethnocentrism, and those elements of superiority which so divide our communities (cf. Eph. 1:23ff.).

In his book, *The Different Drum*, Scott Peck tells an interesting story about how Christians can lead lives of humility which lessen divisions caused by pride in our communities. The story notes how a rabbi and an abbot were working hard to develop their communities. However, after much effort, each was forced to acknowledge the possible failure of their efforts. The rabbi's community and the abbot's monastery nearly closed. Though each institution was in close proximity to the other, their occupants never spoke to each other. They were engaged in their own personal and private dreams. Each group had some knowledge of how to build a community, but what each knew was not sufficient. Because of divergent traditions, they would not talk to each other. So their communities waned and waned. One day, as the abbot talked to his men, who always argued with each other, he told them that he would like to go and visit with the rabbi. They were so shocked that they asked, "Abbot, Why! Since you and the rabbi have nothing in common, how can you speak with him?" So the abbot told them it was his last effort to save his monastery. He persisted and went to see the rabbi without the agreement of his men. He told the rabbi of the difficulty he was experiencing and how his monastery would soon be closed. Then he asked, "What advice can you give to save my monastery?" In a cryptic way, the rabbi replied, "I am not sure what to say except to remind you that one of you at the monastery might be the Messiah." The abbot returned to his men wondering what the rabbi meant by his cryptic remark that "One of you might be the Messiah." The men were surprised to see the abbot come back so soon, and quickly asked, "What did the rabbi say?"   The abbot responded, "He said that one of you might be the Messiah." His men only laughed, for they were sure that none of them was the Messiah. They knew it was not Brother Peter, for he was too impulsive, and it was not Brother Andrew, for he was too cynical, and it was not Brother John, for he was too loud-mouthed. In any case, from that day on, each began to live as if each one were the Messiah, and their little monastery began to grow as others began to see that the Messiah was in the midst of them (*The Different Drum*, pp. 13-15). The point is that each person in the community had come to see that the call of Christ did not mean fitting oneself for individual, personal, private and humanistic honor, but for the living sacrifice or a life of service for God and neighbor.

2.   The Need for Love.

A second principle that must be confronted in the call to community is the need for love. Since we have stated the first principle as the living sacrifice or a life of service, we next turn to love, for, fundamentally, love which is true is sacrificial or self-giving. For Karl Barth, Jesus is the One in whose person God has elected and loved the wider circle of humanity as a whole, but also, with a view to this wider circle, the narrower circle of this special race -- His own community within humanity (*Church Dogmatics*, IV:3, part 2, p. 682). In the lead of the pericope we have been discussing, John also said, "Having loved his own that were in the world, he loved them to the very end." Thus, we insist that the building of community takes love. Leonardo Buscaglia, often referred to as the "Love Doctor," likes to speak of "the politics of love." For he asserts, "We need others to love and we need to be loved by them, only thus can we confront the superficiality of our world. If we do not love we cease to develop, choose madness, and even death" (*Love*, p. 84). According to Paul Tillich, love means the "reunion," "intimacy," and "separation" of "self-centered selves" (*Love, Power and Justice*, pp. 26-27). "Love" is "the ultimate power of union," "the ultimate power over separation," "the infinite which is given to the finite," for it is "stronger than death" (*The New Being*, pp. 58,173,174). Alexis de Tocqueville asserted that self-centeredness (individualism) is the "rust" of contemporary society (*Democracy in America*). The destruction caused by this rust is well stated by Winfred Arn, Carroll Nyquist and Charles Arn:

> For want of Love, a person was lost;
> For want of a person, a family was lost;
> For want of a family, a church was lost;
> For want of a church, a community was lost;
> For want of a community, a city was lost;
> For want of a city, a state was lost;
> For want of a state a nation was lost.
> For want of Love . . . . .
> (*Who Cares About Love*, p.115).

Love, in the biblical perspective, is fundamentally defined as the self-giving (sacrificial) principle of life (*agape*, Jn. 3:16). Other words which appear in the Bible or in secular Greek, such as *philia, eros,* and *storge*, do have their place, but they only find positive significance when they are impacted by *agape*. John reminds us that, "Love is from God" (Jn. 4:7), and it is known from its practical expression. In Paul's words:

> Love is patient; love is kind; love is not envious or boastful or arrogant or rude. It does not insist on its own way; it is not irritable or resentful; it does not rejoice in wrongdoing, but rejoices in the truth. It bears all things, believes all things, hopes all things, endures all things. Love never ends...(1 Cor. 13:4-8).

The creative and redemptive power of love will not allow for inordinate, self-seeking, oppressive, power-over relationships. Some call this "false love" (*eros*), for true love will never engage in intimacy for what it can get out of it, but will break out into creative experiences. For radical liberation theologian Fredrick Herzog, Jesus viewed true love as a call to creative, redemptive, and sacrificial relationships. In showing this love through the act of footwashing, He acted like "a shoe-shine boy." So we may follow His command to love to the very end: "A new commandment I give to you that you should love one another as I have loved you" (*Liberation Theology*, p. 179).

Churches that have learned to share love will sacrifice for the upbuilding of humanity. For church growth specialists, love in Jesus' name attracts people and is the best form of evangelism (cf. Winfred Arn, et al., *Who Cares about Love?*). If the love offered by churches were to stop with their members, they would find it relatively easy to love. However, love moves us into enemy territory, to strangers and enemies, to celebrate the brotherhood and sisterhood of humanity. This is where love can be tested. As "a gift," "a fruit," a holy potential, love makes us overcome our prejudices and our hatred, and helps us to confront ugliness, stupidity, fear, and rejection. The one who professes devotion to God abides in love. That is why, when the devil seeks to tear us apart and lead us to the abuse of power which seeks to destroy us, we can say "No, we will not allow such destruction for He who has called us wills us to love."

3. The Need for Obedience

The third principle on which we must focus is obedience. R. E. O. White notes it well that love is associated with obedience (_The Night He Was Betrayed_, p. 69). And obedience must be added to love, for in a culture where self lacks control, we must note the impact of a love that can be commanded and a love which controls us. When Jesus said, "If you love me keep my commandments" (Jn. 4:15), He struck at the heart of the grasping for power which the children of disobedience know well. To be obedient is to risk not saying "I," or refusing to grasp for a little more power when such is possible through the manipulation of others. To be obedient is to accept "submission" to "the will to God" as Jesus submitted His will to His Father's will. Submission is a word much misunderstood today, and I shall note reasons for its misunderstanding later, but here, it means sharing power as Jesus shared power with His disciples. To submit is to accept the vocation of discipleship. In effect, submissive obedience challenges the success mentality which has so dominated our culture. William Barclay says it beautifully that if a person sets out on the Christian way, it is the end of self. That person can no longer please herself/himself. Instead, she/he must also place herself/himself entirely under the orders of Jesus Christ. Again, if a person sets out on the Christian way, it is the end of the world's scale of values. While the world assesses the value of a person by the material things she/he possesses or by the power she/he wields, Christianity values a person by what she/he gives away and the service she/he gives. Again, if a person sets out on the Christian way, she/he has a new scale of loyalties, and as such, she/he sets out on a life in which Christ and His principles (humility, love, and submission) come first (*And Jesus Said*, pp. 206-208).

Three Forms of Community

I have spoken of community in a certain way and revealed its potency for great spiritual blessings and its potency for destruction. My initial conclusion is that out of this we can articulate three forms of community in the Church, namely:

a.   There is a horizontal - humanistic view of community in which the evil powers reign. Such a community operates on a plain of flatness where human only meets human.

Human  Human

In this community there is no spirit of humility and no service to humanity, only self-interest.

b.   Then there is an individualistic, privatistic, autonomous community which seeks its own end. It does show some God-like interest and is sometimes vertical,

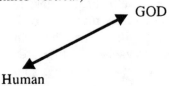
GOD

Human

but its basic thrust is pretentious, pharisaical, and indifferent to human needs. I shall say much more about the spirit of this form of community in another chapter of this text, but for now, I think R. E. O. White's record of J. R. Clements' reflection on the traitor at the table of the Lord's Supper, as recorded in John 13, illustrates this spirit,

> Someone is slighting the Savior-
> Lord is it I?
> Someone is spurning His love once again-
> Lord is it I?
> Someone is living in selfish delight-
> Lord is it I?
> Someone is turning his face from the light-
> Lord is it I?
> Someone's betraying his master today-
> Lord is it I?
> Some one is walking a perilous way-
> Lord is it I?
> (See, _The Night He Was Betrayed_, pp. 48-49).

In a way, the form of community I here illustrate seeks to latch on to God, but in the end it reveals its evil in a personality cult which knows no repentance (_Metanoia_) nor humility of mind (_Tapeinophron_).

c. Finally, there is a Community of the Spirit in which Christ reigns. Its directions are both vertical and horizontal, and are connected in the circumference of the cross.

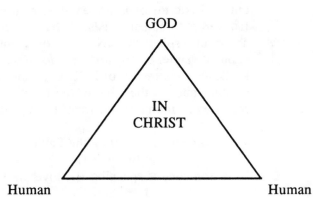

Here the Lordship of Christ inspires the humility, love, and obedience that make community. As Gary Collins would have us understand, the Christian who seeks community:

► Consistently acknowledges God's sovereignty and power.
► Seeks to please God (2 Cor. 5:9).
► Serves God, does good deeds, cares for, builds up, and encourages others to be God-like (Gal. 5:13; 6:9,10; 1 Cor. 12:25; 1 Thess. 5:11).
► Does not strive for status, acclaim, riches or possessions.
► Trusts God to provide for all needs.
► Humbly recognizes, accepts, develops, and uses God-given gifts, strengths, and abilities.
► Does not resist being used by God, even if it means the accumulation of worldly goods and status.
► Avoids jealousy or coveting a position of prominence and realizes that God gives responsibilities, gifts, and status as He wills (Ps. 75:5-7; 1 Cor. 12:4-18; Gal. 5:24-26); and is

aware of the fact that dedicated service to God does not always bring worldly success - sometimes, persecution and hardship result instead (Heb. 11:32-40) (_Beyond Easy Believism_, p. 97).

Every time I look at Leonardo da Vinci's painting of the "Last Supper," I see in it the three forms of communities just illustrated. Though we might not be able to perfect it in our world, yet we should pray that the church which is the True Church will understand the contradictions, and seek through the grace of God to approximate the Community for which Christ prayed, "Sanctify them in the truth, Your word is truth" (Jn. 17:17). In response to the question which Martin Luther King, Jr. asked three decades ago, "_Where do we go from here: chaos or community?_" God's people should respond: "COMMUNITY!" For in every moment of genuine love, we are dwelling in God and God in us (Paul Tillich, _The New Being_, p. 29).

CHAPTER THREE

LEADERS AS EMPOWERERS:
True Servants in the Community

Confronting the Pecking Order Syndrome

According to Richard Foster, a group of people cannot be together for very long until a "pecking order" is clearly established. He points to this fact as a social phenomenon noticeable in such things as where people sit, how they walk in relation to each other, who always gives way when two people are walking at the same time, who stands back when a job needs to be done, and who steps forward. "These things," he says, "are written on the face of human society" ("The Ministry of the Towel: Practicing Love through Service," *Christianity Today*, Jan. 7, 1983, pp. 18-21). We must agree that Foster is somehow correct, for we see it every day. But as Foster notes, the footwashing celebration seeks to challenge that social fact.

On the basis of the above observation, our present discussion will seek to deal with the reality of leadership which over-emphasizes hierarchy - ranking and ordering. It will deal with those forms of relationships that create competition and control while neglecting the service which builds community. I will focus on the fact that while human community is built upon power relationships, relationships in

the church - especially at the level of leadership - should reflect loving service at the center of all relationships. The point being made is that footwashing teaches us that the whole church is under the Lordship of Christ and is subject to Christ's Spirit Who gives His gifts for the life and leadership of the community. In church leadership, therefore, we need to place a greater emphasis on our loving service to God rather than on the privilege of the positions in which we find ourselves. We need to challenge the kind of leadership which does not think of others in community in the context of collegiality but as steps at the bottom to be walked upon. A friend of mine described it well when he said, "The higher on the organizational chart - the better." And it is a great tragedy that, even in the church as a community, we work under the guise of piety, to peddle our positions and privileges for selfish advantage, control, personal attention, and display.
Instead of behaving as servants and doing things to bring blessings to others, we work for the benefit of ourselves.
The footwashing experience in John 13 is the classic example of what community leadership should mean. It is the interpretation of Christ's word, "Let the one who is greatest among you be the one who serves." The key point is that we need to challenge our paradigms of power in which God is sometimes at the top, men just below, then women, children, and other living creatures at the bottom. Footwashing is - for me - the contradiction of this common culture, since it leads all in the community to act as "footwashers," as servants of God and as servants of one another.

Community and Service Leadership

       The model of leadership that it sets forth is a leadership of service. It can be so focused because it is spiritually determined and challenges a one-person or authoritarian show. It focuses on the reality of giftedness and the value of the whole community. It emphasizes humility (submission), love, and obedience.

Jesus articulated the most beautiful model of leadership to the apostles, especially when He said,

> You know that among the Gentiles those whom they recognize as their rulers lord it over them, and their great ones are tyrants over them. But it is not so among you, but whoever wishes to become great among you must be your servant, and whoever wishes to be first among you must be slave of all. For the Son of Man came not to be served but to serve, and to give His life a ransom for many (Mk. 10:42-45 paraphrased).

The emphasis is not on position, status, and high prestige, but on loving obedience of service. The creation of reality comes through incarnation. Instead of a leadership of manipulation, oppression, and self-aggrandizement, one can find a leadership of encouragement, vision, and liberation. In Jesus' framework these ideas of leadership are not minor matters. Rather, they are to be seen as the potent resources from which community is built. I shall take these up under the rubric of _who_ a leader is and what a leader _does_.

Who the Leader is: The Qualities of Leadership

When one reads through the Bible, one finds that much emphasis is placed on _who_ a leader is. I shall discuss this first because what happens for a community often happens because of _who_ its leader is. The sad commentary at the end of the book of the Judges is that "In those days there was no king in Israel: all the people did that which was right in their eyes" (Judges 21:25). To make such the central point for a book is not commendable, and the stories in the book demonstrate the harsh reality of poor leadership. Now, one should not suspect that correct behavior requires some judge or king as leader, but the point to be held in view is that leadership does impact community behavior, and the moral and spiritual qualities of a leader are important here. When Jesus called His disciples and sought to prepare for building the new community, He first laid emphasis on their spiritual lives as leaders. I have therefore decided to take these up as (1) leadership and charismatic power; (2) leadership and humility; and (3) leadership and obedience.

1. *Leadership and Charismatic Power*

Several years ago, sociologist Max Weber defined the main quality of leadership as "charisma," that is, a "gift of grace," which is either inherited or offered to a person by others. On the basis of such a definition, leadership has often focussed on the unique qualities of a person (power) rather than the obedient, sacrificial service to which a person is called. The one qualified to lead has been named for his/her (presumed) supernatural competencies (power) such as great speaking ability or some defined quality given by group decision (*Economy and Society: An Outline of Interpretative Sociology*, p. 241ff.). We can name a lot of such leaders, "good" and "bad," whose leadership has not been judged by moral or spiritual competence but by personality (power). For Richard Quebedeaux, in this age of electronic technology, most persons who lead do not actually possess "supernatural endowments," but are made to appear so by the media (*By*

What Authority, p.117).   And these kinds of leaders are especially sought after when our culture is in need of messiahs. By accepting prestige and personality as a definition of leadership, church people tend to forget their divine dependence, and they turn to public ratings to find the *who* would be made leader. According to a radio commentary, one of the colleagues of Jim Baker confessed, "At P.T.L. we just stopped praying and trusting God, while the show just kept going on, and our inordinate affections led us to make tragic decisions, and soon there was a scandal."

Now, charisma means *power* and power is a gift of God, but when charisma as power is emptied of its spiritual meaning, it only maintains a this-worldly bearing, and leads people to use their magical, demonic magnetism, intense coercive force, and the offering of prizes, awards, ribbons, and honorific offices for the maintenance of personal power (cf. William J. Goode, *The Celebration of Heroes: Prestige as a Social Control System*).   This was very much displayed in Hitler's Germany and is used often in more subtle ways for the maintenance of power in small groups and communities. Correctly understood, "charisma" is "a gift of the divine Spirit," "a gift of grace," (*charis*) which makes a person sense the presence of God, and it fills one with faith, wisdom, love, and courage.   According to the Biblical notes on the early church, everyone who led was first and foremost charismatically gifted with faith, wisdom, and the power to love (Cf. Acts 2:1-4; 6:1-7; 1 Tim. 3; 2 Tim. 2:1-7; Titus 1:7-9). I emphasize this fact for, when God calls a community into being and sets forth leadership in that community, such leadership is to be the fruitage of the Spirit and not just popularity contests. Leadership here is not to be judged on the basis of prestige and personality in a worldly sense, but on the basis of the authority (*exousia* and *dunamis*) given by the Spirit.

2. *Leadership and Humility*

Our perspective on charisma directs us again to the words of Jesus, that "The one who wants to be greatest must be like the one that serves." The idea is that the leader of the Christian community must be conscious that leadership does not begin with lust - that is, a grasping for power, a desire to be seen, or just wanting to be in charge - but a consciousness of loyalty to God and faithfulness to God's people. Loyalty to God means dedication of heart and life to discipleship and servanthood. Disciples do not seek to draw attention to themselves, or work to create a favorable impression about themselves. Instead, they live in faithfulness as servants of Christ. The biblical words for "servant" (*diakonos* and *doulos*) which we have been noting, are basically translated as "minister" and "slave," but each word has much broader meanings. Fundamentally, *diakonos* is a servant at the table, but the term has been used for those who shared the word (Acts 6:4; Phil. 1:1). However, the word which is quite attractive is *doulos*, for it was more often used by the apostles as identifying their bonding to their Lord and their unity with God's people (Rom. 1:1; Phil. 1:1; Titus 1:1: 2 Pet. 1:1; Jude 1:1; Rev. 1:1). Jesus Himself used the word to speak of His identification with humanity (Matt. 12:18; Isa. 42:1; 52:13; 53:11; Phil. 2:5-8).

This emphasis on servanthood was not new, for the prophets, from Moses, the great leader and law-giver (Deut. 34:5; Ps. 105:26; Mal. 4:4), to Joshua, the great commander (Joshua 24:29), and David, the greatest king in Israel (2 Sam. 3:18; Ps. 78:70), were servants of God. The word also carries profound social implications. William Barclay comments that masters did what they liked with their *doulos* in the ancient world, even possessing the power of life and death over them, so, in like manner, the lives of God's servants belong to God.

As in the ancient world slaves had no rights, for all their rights were surrendered to their masters, so the _doulos_ of God must be aware that they owe an unquestioning obedience to God. As in the ancient world, a master's command was the only law known to a slave, and the slave could only ask, "Master, what will you have me to do?"   So the _doulos_ of God must be constantly in the service of God.   As in the ancient world, slaves literally had no time of their own, no holidays, no leisure;   all their time belonged to their masters,   so the _doulos_ of God must neither deliberately nor unconsciously compartmentalize their lives and activities into that which belongs to God and that which does not belong to God (William Barclay, _The Letters of James and Peter_, pp. 292, 293).   The servant (_diakonos_ or _doulos_) of God belongs to God, but we should not over-emphasize the metaphor of servanthood as if God has slaves. For slavery or service with God, as Paul makes clear in the Epistle to the Romans, is not servility but freedom; neither is it oppressive but a voluntary act of faith. To lead as God's servant is to recognize this faith relationship as God's gift. That means to be able to see every child of God with dignity and integrity as the Creator sees them.

Here, I find the necessity to insist upon the connection between _charisma_ and _doulos_ (giftedness and service) because of the human tendency to use charisma as a "divine right" and means of self-authentication. As _charisma_ challenges a leader to authority and power, _doulos_ calls that leader to faithfulness in service.   A contemporary understanding of "servant leadership" has received special consideration from Robert K. Greenleaf, who calls it "a journey into the nature of legitimate power and greatness." In the first chapter of his book _Servant Leadership_, which is a collection of his speeches, he speaks of "the individual" who is called to lead, but who must recognize that the first qualification for leadership is the willingness to serve. In a later chapter, he argues that every church ought to have some positive individuals who will take the lead in service, not a few *negative* individuals, but a few *positive* individuals. People who can enlarge the vision and liberate the community and who will reach their highest fulfillment through serving and being served, using service as a common venture, are servant leaders.   Such individuals, he notes, must understand that the task of the Church is not just to focus outside of itself and say the problems of society are "out there" and not "in here."   And they must see that if they desire to make a change in the world, they must begin "in here," *in* the Church.   Greenleaf believes that not everyone will be true servants, as we have described them, but he argues that those who are servants must take the lead and serve so that others will follow in service.   The question of status is diminished, for though the basic definition of a leader is "one who goes before others," leadership of discipleship and servanthood is not privilege, but responsibility.

3.   Leadership and Obedience

Privilege calls for responsibility.   Responsibility calls for accountability.   Accountability calls for commitment. Commitment calls for obedience.   Obedience, according to John Yoder, is to take the servant stance in society, to lead people to Christ instead of leading them to self-praise and hero worship (cf. *The Politics of Jesus*, pp. 244-248). Few individuals are immune to the power which flows from high profile personalities.   So it takes obedience to Jesus for those in power to control their authority.   For Rudolf Bultmann, obedience calls people away from subjugation to external authority to the worship of the one true God (*Jesus and the Word*, p. 76).   I speak then of the discipline of obedience as responding to the command of Jesus, "Do to others as I have done to you."

Since leadership is challenged by the external, immediate glory dominant in society, we focus on that leadership which walked the servant's road. We find effective leadership where the glory of God shines in Jesus Christ.

People who lust for leadership or who have an overbearing ambition to lead do not understand this servant's road. Jesus could speak of John the Baptist as among the greatest of humans ever born of women, because John knew what it meant not to call attention to himself, but to point to the Lamb of God who would take away the sins of the world. With profound sincerity John said, "He will increase, but I must decrease." Not for a moment did John ever try to use his powers for his own interests. His mission was to be a forerunner of Christ and that is what he did -- perfectly.

If there is a basis on which obedience rests, it is this self-less interest. The significance of "If you love me, you will keep my commandments" (John 14:15) and "I give you a new commandment that you love one another" (John 13:34) is that we are called to focus on Christ instead of self. In fact, it is said the power of Christ's life is that He never once called attention to Himself. He always pointed people to God. "I must do the will of the One who sent me and finish His work."

What Leadership Does

If "who a leader is" is the first question of importance, "what a leader does" follows, for who a leader is might stand hidden, but the actions of a leader are always visible for public scrutiny. I classify this dimension of leadership under three captions, namely:

(1) Leadership empowers people.
(2) Leadership encourages people.

(3)   Leadership builds unity among people.

The leadership which does these three things acknowledges that its power (*exousia, dunamis* and *kratus*) is not ultimate power (authority, dynamics and strength), but that its power resides in God and is shared with God's people.

(1)   *Leadership as Empowerment*

I begin with empowerment as one of the first tasks of a leader, for it is notable that the single most important dimension of charismatic leadership is the leaders' ability to share their consciousness of spirit, so that the goals and objectives of a community are not the leaders' possessions, but are defined in a communal perspective. In the context of the spiritual community, the charismatic leader leads people under the vision of Christ. That means power is shared, instead of hoarded and kept from the weak and powerless.

Empowerment in the kingdom of God means that ordinary people will share power and participate actively in the work of God. For power is not alone in the hands of ministers and priests or clergy and elders, but in the hands of all of God's people.

In developing an empowerment program for aiding people to participate in their live's processes in his Glide Memorial Church in San Francisco, Pastor Cecil Williams suggests the following:

(a)   Empowerment begins with authenticity, that is, helping people to discover their inner spiritual source of power.

(b)   Empowerment requires claiming ownership of one's own culture and life; that is, to declare one's identity from one's own context.

(c)   Empowerment comes in knowing that one has power but acknowledging that such power is not

ultimate. This means God is the Ultimate power.
(d)   Empowerment is measured by the good it offers to
"the extended family." That means acknowledging
the reality of the constant partnership that we have
in community (*No Hiding Place*, pp. 59-64).

Williams' work has to do with addicts and abused people,
but every leader of a spiritual community needs to learn from
him that empowerment is a necessity if the whole community
is to be activated to live spiritually and authentically.

(1a). *Leadership as Management*

As a subcategory of empowerment I focus on
management, for it is on the management side of leadership
that charismatic leadership is tested. Leaders in our culture of
specialization are trained to control and manage their
environment. Those who cannot manage and control are seen
as ineffective leaders. But often enough it is managing and
controlling that destroy community. So how can leaders of the
spiritual community manage in a way that their leadership is
empowering instead of manipulative and oppressive? One can
only insist that the model is offered by Jesus. In His teachings,
Jesus focused many parables on management (Luke 16:2-4;
Matt. 24:45-51; Matt. 25:14ff). And these parables show that
He had no conflict with management for His managers were
always servants. So, it is to misconstrue the whole idea of
good servanthood that we despise the idea of management in
the Church. Michael T. Dibbert believes that churches
struggle with management-related issues because few leaders
are trained to deal with the management responsibilities they
encounter. Seminaries, for example, offer very few courses
in church management, and even if seminaries did offer many
courses, pastoral trainees would pass by them because they are

educated to think that they went to seminary to learn to preach, teach, and be "fishers of men" (Matt. 4:19). An even greater reason the Church suffers from such poor management is that many successful business people who lead in the church do not think of the church in the same way they think of their businesses. They do not employ the same management skills they use in their businesses when it comes to managing the church. Many successful business people are not great managers of practical communities like the Church (*Spiritual Leadership*, pp. 20-22). My contention is that church people do not need to fear good management since good management simply means a just and effective leadership.

(1b). *Leadership as Equipping*

In conjunction with empowerment I also speak in traditional terms of leadership as equipping. For one of the greatest tasks of charismatic leadership, what Jane Howell and Bruce Avolio call the ethical task of charismatic leadership, is to consider the aspirations and leadership potential of followers ("The Ethics of Charismatic Leadership: Submission or Liberation?" *The Academy of Management Executive,* vol.6:2, May 1992, p. 43). Jesus called, equipped, and commissioned His disciples for their work. In light of such understanding, we should mourn for those churches that are so poorly equipped and commissioned that they cannot render any effective service. By commissioning, I mean affirming people with their gifts and allowing them freedom to lead. Instead of leaving communities without a constant supply of leaders, commissioning makes it possible for others to lead. As I think of the difficulty of women getting into ministry, I share the conviction that it is not that God's gifts are not given to all of God's people, but it is that those who are in positions of power and should commission women have often been unwilling to do this commissioning.

Equipping leadership acknowledges the charismatic structure of the church and shifts the focus from the "supermen" to all who are called and gifted by God. When the author of Timothy stated, "Do not neglect the gift (_charisma_) that is in you" (1 Tim. 4:14), he did not mean it for Timothy alone, but for all of God's people - men and women, alike. As the Scriptures show, the diversity of gifts is calculated for the leading and upbuilding of the body.

I name the following as examples of such gifts:

SERVICE	COMMUNITY BUILDING	WITNESSING
Giving Aid	Exhortation	Prophecy
		Rom. 12:6-8
Acts of mercy	Liberality	Teaching
Healing	Discernment	Wisdom
		1 Cor. 12:4-11
Miracles	Interpretation	Knowledge
Faith	Edification	Prophecy
		Tongues
	Pastors and	Apostles
	Teachers	Eph. 4:11
	Prophets	
	Evangelists	
Serving	Serving	Speaking
		1 Pet. 4:11

Again, the distribution of gifts states that no one person -man or woman - can claim to have all the potential for leadership, for in community the focus is not so much on the charismatic person as it is on the charismatic community.

(2) *Leadership as Encouragement*

The leadership which delegates authority, equips people, and affirms them is a leadership of encouragement. Encouragement is important because it includes giving advice, motivation, energizing, and, as Paul said it, "We who are strong ought to put up with the failings of the weak and not to please ourselves" (Rom. 15:1). One of the greatest gifts of the Spirit is encouragement, and leadership is offered a share in this activity.

The leader who encourages cares. Caring demands that a leader takes notice of the little things as they impact the lives of people. The "little things" are defined by Richard Foster as "service of hiddenness," "service of small things," "service of guarding the reputation of others," "service of being served," "service of courtesy," "service of hospitality," "service of listening," "service of bearing the burdens of each other," and "service of sharing the word of life" (see "The Ministry of the Towel: Practicing Love Through Service," *Christianity Today*, Jan. 7, 1993, pp.18-21). This encouraging/caring is truly the context in which one understands leadership as a call to the death of self for it means putting the needs of other persons before ours, and it means loving to the very end. In short, there are caring leaders and parasitic leaders. There are burden bearers and leaders that feed on others. The latter help Satan to build his dominion of chaos while the former build up the kingdom of God.

(3) *Leadership as Building Unity Among People*

The third task of leadership is unity building, and I note its critical importance in this case, for I am saying that the community of which I speak is called into being by Christ, but that its history has an earthly orientation. Those who are part of it through their individuality and difference often run contrary to their real focus of unity with Christ.

In the footwashing of John 13 and the intercessory prayer of John 17, Jesus pressed for unity because He knew that the sinister spirit of disunity was present among His disciples. And it was not until Pentecost that the group of disciples approximated the unity for which Christ prayed (Acts 2; 4:32f.). In any case, unity became a major theme of their ministry. Over and over, they exhorted their churches to _pray_ and _work_ for unity. And when Paul joined the apostles, he constantly reminded his congregations to live in unity. To the Christians of Rome, he notes that though they are many, they are _one_ body, and they need to have _one_ mind (Rom. 12:4,16).   He challenges the Christians of Corinth to be mindful that though they have differing qualities and gifts, they are members of _one_ body (1 Cor. 12:12-31). Gifts are from _one_ Spirit. All are belonging to the _one_ God. Quarreling Christians are reminded that in the community there should be no divisions among them (1 Cor. 1:10). Those who strive constantly must understand that they are living according to the principles of "the flesh" and not according to "the Spirit" (1 Cor. 3:3). When immorality is causing division, Paul even shows that the leader should lead out in excommunication (1 Cor. 5; 2 Cor. 5). The point is that Christians are to maintain the unity of the Spirit in the bond of peace (Eph. 4:3-6).

The other apostles in their epistles all agree that unity is never a spiritual luxury but is essential and true for the development of the Church. The more seriously we take the New Testament, the more urgent and persistent will become our prayers and striving for peace and unity. That does not mean we will pray for a "drab uniformity" of the sort beloved by bureaucrats. But we will pray for a unity in which

powerful tensions are held together by the leadership of the
Spirit. Leadership in spiritual community must set an example
of what unity means in Christ (William Barclay, *The Letters of
James and Peter*, pp. 224-226).

The Lordship of Christ and the Leadership of the Spirit

What we have been insisting on all along is that effective
leadership in the community is under the Lordship of Christ
and the Leadership of the Spirit. Leaders who receive their
authority from Christ will model Christ. They need not turn
to subtle means of manipulation to find authentication. If
Christ calls them into leadership, they will lead, and when
Christ asks them to share power, they will share.

Lawrence O. Richards says it well, that the leadership of
Christian community lives in this consciousness that Jesus is
Lord and that the community is Christ's (Lawrence O.
Richards, *The Theology of Church Leadership*).   When we
think this way, we will not seek for a monopoly on power, but
we will lead with the humility which comes from Christ. In
discussing forms of church government which seek to usurp the
authority of Christ, Karl Barth suggests that those who
proclaim the authority of Jesus Christ should recognize Him
and His Spirit as the creator and guarantor of unity. He is the
guarantee in the matter, and no one should presuppose that
there is to be any other besides Him (*Church Dogmatics* IV.1,
p. 674).

We take to this as our point of departure and accept it as
our conclusion, for Christ is first and last in everything. He is
the Head and Lord over all. He is Lord or not at all. Under
His Lordship and His leadership, we can build communities of
servants and friends where everyone together experiences the
conditions necessary for developing more powerful selves.

CHAPTER FOUR

CELEBRATING THE BOND BETWEEN US: Mutuality in the Community

A Paradigm of Mutuality

When Jesus concluded the act of footwashing with His disciples, He did not finish without comment. In order to emphasize His example, He told them that they should do to each other as He had done for them (John 13:13,14). This, for me, is a beautiful paradigm of mutuality, for it does not put one person up, and another, down. It does not ask one person to be lord, and another, servant. It does not make one person boss, and another, slave. It does not make community possible for the strong and exclude the weak. It does not welcome the rich and drive away the poor. It does not set up a ruling class and destroy an under class. But it does follow the strategy of Jesus where He notes that life means the experiencing of God and neighbor --together (Matt. 5:43-48). That is, the experiencing of a blessed freedom of the Spirit which is radically opposed to any authoritarian principles and powers which rule the world is what distinguishes the Church from the world as community.

In a review of Juan Segundo's view of footwashing, Tom Driver argues that footwashing is the "God-present experience" in which the Spirit draws near and presses believers together (*The Magic of Rituals*, pp. 204-208). Thus, we can say that mutuality, as it is focused through footwashing, cuts out the "dog eat dog" model by which the world operates, and replaces it by extoling the virtues of intimacy, confidence, security, respect, honesty, interchange, and mutual- or inter-dependency (see, *The Random House Dictionary of the English Language*, 2nd. ed., 1987). Aspects of mutuality like "mutual dependency" are getting a "bad rap" in our "culture of individualism" today. In any case, whereas we see co-dependency as destructive to life and productive of dysfunctional churches (cf. M. Crosby, "The Dysfunctional Church," *Other Side*, 28, Jan/Feb 1992, pp. 40-41), we see mutuality and inter-dependency as positive to life's development and important for Spiritual community. By mutual inter-dependency, I speak of *koinonia* (communion, sharing, reciprocal support, and partnership), which does not grasp at personal interests but thinks in the biblical sense of the interests of others. Although the word *koinonia* is not found in the Gospels, as a concept it is dominant throughout them. And it helps us to challenge the abusive processes that cause us to play class distinction games or make us participate in racism, sexism, or individualism. In place of the radical individualism which dominates our culture, I fell the need to issue a call for a revival of mutuality.

In his book, *Criterion for the Church*, J. Robert Nelson highlights mutuality in community when he reviews the work of Swiss theologian, Philippe H. Menoud, who notes that in the context of ecclesiology:

(a)   There is a spiritual meaning of *koinonia* which draws attention to "the tie that binds our hearts in Christian love." It focuses on the unity of the Spirit in the bond of peace. In its double path, it mediates the love of God in

Jesus Christ through the power of the Spirit. It calls attention to participation in the love of community, brotherhood/sisterhood, and neighbor, and urges Christians to share together in the new life of the Spirit which is both a possibility and a reality under the rulership of Christ.

(b)   There is a material meaning of *koinonia* which points to the New Testament experience where "all had things in common." The emphasis here is that people were willing to share their material possessions so that the economic needs of all members were supplied through the voluntary and unconditional surrender of property for the common good.

(c)   There is an ecclesiastical meaning of *koinonia* in which mutual support in the church is of absolute importance. In the New Testament churches the members gave visible and tangible evidence that they belonged to one another because they all suffered with the needs of each other.

(d)   And there is a eucharistic meaning of *koinonia* in which the community can share in "the breaking of bread." In this sense the community is called the body of Christ. The fellowship around and in Christ is that which brings mutuality. Any false practice of the eucharist which betrays Christ can be criticized. For example, Paul asks, "The cup of blessing that we bless, is it not a sharing (*koinonia*) in the blood of Christ? The bread we break, is it not a participation (*koinonia*) in the body of Christ?" (1 Cor. 10:16).

The point is that *koinonia* creates mutuality and intimacy. The latter is to be articulated alongside of mutuality, for it is intimacy which builds mutual-dependency, and mutual-dependency which builds community. In a mutual community such as the Church, we are not just blood relatives, but we are an extended family who - through faith in the blood of Christ - understand that the principle of intimacy is not egotistic or individualistic, but is self-less in service for the growth and development of others.   We hold it that the blood of Jesus Christ (1 John 1:7-9) creates a new order of humanity which runs counter to parochialism and self-centered salvation.

In the context of biblical theology, we point out that relationship in the community is Christ-centered, but not just in a mystical way.   For connection with Christ immediately connects with the Father and with the Father's people.   Martin Buber, who displayed great interest in community, has shown in a debate with Martin Heideger and Soren Kierkegaard that the true followers and imitators of God understand their relationship to the world of human beings, their relationship to themselves, and their relationship to mystery.   They do not need to reject the world community to seek God, for God is God in relationship -- not just for one, but for all of us (see *Between Man and Man,* pp. 175-181).   The New Testament is very insistent with this, that *God is for us,   Christ is for us,* and that no one can stake a claim on Christ without including others.   Therefore, we can insist that there is no authentic mutuality apart from Christ.   Christ, as we shall indicate, often mediates the mysteries of life (John 15-17).   Through Him we can break out of our individualism and self-serving interests for our family, friends, and churches and be open to the mutuality that is in the world.   And whereas we will emphasize the latter in another discussion,   I cannot yet leave the focus on intimacy for the Church, for it is from the strength of intimacy that we build community for the world.

According to Jurgen Moltmann, lack of relationship is ultimately our affliction in the Church (*The Power of the Powerless,* p. 100).   So, the language and practice of mutuality is not superfluous.   Letty Russell says,

> Only with a principle of mutuality can human persons truly be affirmed as embodied subjects; as beings whose value lies not only in their freedom but also in their capacity to know and be known, to love and be loved; as beings whose destiny is communion (Ann Loades, editor, _Feminist Interpretation of the Bible_, p. 47).

As a caveat, I might note that there are some things about the gender interpretation of the Scriptures that might be arguable. In any case, one cannot deny that some of their interpretations have brought profound consciousness to aspects of theology that stress community, intimacy, and mutuality. On such a basis I use conscious gender interpretations in parts of this discussion to point out that the understanding of mutuality can strengthen our Christian community. For whereas we live in times when it is acceptable to be cynical of intimacy, we have a new opportunity through the strong gender critique to articulate our respect for each other, our equality with each other, and our will to live in freedom with each other.

A Theology of Mutuality for Community

My reading of the Scriptures shows that where love as _agapé_ is understood, there are no illusions with regard to a theology of mutuality. Inasmuch as I speak of the New Testament as focusing on the Gospel as a movement from the intimate community, yet in a number of passages it is noted that we should:

Be devoted to one another (Rom. 12:10).
Be of the same mind to one another (Rom. 12:16).

Do not judge one another (Rom. 14:13).
Pursue the things which make for peace for the building
    up of one another (Rom. 14:19).
Love one another (Jn. 13:34; 15:12; 15:17; Rom. 13:8;
    1 Thess. 4:9; 1 Pet. 1:22; 1 Jn. 3:11; 1 Jn. 4:7).
Forgive one another (Eph. 4:32; Col. 3:13).
Do not oppress one another (Lev. 25:14,17).
Serve one another (Gal. 5:13).
Be compassionate to one another (Rom. 12:10;
    Eph. 4:32).
Greet one another (Rom. 16:16; 1 Cor. 16:20;
    2 Cor. 13:12; 1 Pet. 5:14).
Teach one another (Col. 3:16; 1 Thess. 5:11).
Admonish one another (Col. 3:16; Rom. 15:14).
Comfort one another (1 Thess. 4:18).
Bear one another's burdens (Gal. 6:2).
Exhort one another (Heb. 3:13; 10:25).
Consider one another (Heb. 10:24).
Accept one another (Rom. 15:7).
Care for one another (1 Cor. 12:25).
Speak to one another in psalms, hymns, and
    spiritual songs (Eph. 5:18-21).
Stimulate one another to love and good deeds
    (Heb. 10:22-25).
Do not speak against one another (James 4:11).
Confess your sins to one another and pray for one
    another (James 5:16).
Be hospitable to one another (1 Peter 4:9).
Clothe yourselves with humility toward one another
    (1 Peter 5:5).

These instructions are not superfluous, for the people who belong to Christ are to be mutually useful to one another, mutually tender, wearing the badge of mutual love. The emphasis in discipleship is that mutuality is not optional. As

Barth would maintain, "From the very outset Jesus Christ did not envisage individual followers, disciples, and witnesses, but a plurality of such united by Him both with Himself and with one another (*Church Dogmatics*, IV:3, Part 2, p. 681). We are baptized into one Lord, into one Spirit, and into one body. So what mutuality means is partnership in community. Letty Russell would have us understand that "We can only learn to be partners by being partners" (*Growth in Partnership*, p. 39). The biblical point is that spiritual mutuality moves beyond self-interest to an overflow of life which gives itself in self-sacrifice. The issue that leads us to this reflection is the words of Jesus.

So if I, your Lord and Teacher, have washed your feet, you also ought to wash one another's feet. For I have set you an example that you also should do as I have done to you. Very truly, I tell you, servants are not greater than their master; nor are messengers greater than the one who sent them. If you know these things, you are blessed if you do them (John 13:14-17).

In looking, then, at the significance of mutuality, I will emphasize some things which are to be learned today:

1. *Mutuality helps us emphasize the relevance of communion and communication.*

When we state the significance of communication for the Church (implying that church members need to learn communication skills), people most often get the idea that what we intend is that they should take a course in public speaking for sharing the Gospel. But maybe our greatest weakness is that we do not even know how to speak with God or with each other. Speech and language, as we know, are developed in intimate community, not because of any course of study, but because of association. So I stress that the mutuality of community is significant for the development of communication.

It also needs to be restated that it is communication that creates community. In the theological understanding of things, God communicates with us through *revelation*; we communicate with God through ritual, prayer, tears, meditation, and song. And we communicate with each other in the community of faith through the sharing of friendship, fun, and fellowship. "We share our mutual woes, our mutual burdens bear, and often for each other flows the sympathizing tear" (John Fawcett, 1772). These mutual sharings are formally spoken of as *communion* (as shared in the symbols of bread and wine), the *communion of saints* (as shared in the fellowship), and the *grammar of the liturgy* (as shared in the worship).

Whatever formal formulation we give to the above, the point is that in the Church as mutual community (*koinonia*), we learn the possibility of making effective communion and communication. We learn that for communion and communication to take place, the barrier of sin and all the cultural barriers which divide us as persons must be broken down. We learn the necessity of infinite condescension -- 'the coming down of God.' We learn that communication means 'childlikeness of spirit.' And we learn the meaning of submission. Before we briefly address the subject of submission, here is the point being made about communion and communication: namely, that whereas in the world people speak with "I" and "you," in mutual community the emphasis leads to "we" and "us."

2. *Mutuality helps us grasp the essence of submission.*

One of the most studied concepts these days is "submission." I think it needs some clear analysis, because when it is used, an emotion develops that stands in contradiction to love. Earlier, I hinted that communion and communication demand submission. Now, I propose that - from the biblical perspective - submission is one of the most crucial community words. For individuals who have little respect for the Scriptures, submission is a difficult concept. But it needs to be noted that the ideas of submission and incarnation are conjoined. For God to communicate with us, there must have been submission on the part of God (Phil. 2:5-8). He must have bent down. Therefore, submission, has positive significance for our understanding of community.

In an analysis of submission in the context of family "house code" (*Haustafalen*), as is laid out in the Scriptures, John Yoder notes that submission has a revolutionary character, because:

1. It lets people on the bottom side of a social scale be addressed with the same dignity as those in supposed positions of control.
2. It allows those who are tempted to be non-subordinate to remember that God calls all persons in community to humility.
3. It acknowledges that those living together live on a basis of charity (*agape*), rather than on a basis of rules and regulations.
4. It points out that dominant people in relationships can humble themselves.
5. It demonstrates that, within community, people can respect each other's freedom as God in covenant

respects everyone's freedom.
6. It focuses on the fact that with the community of love, a whole new order of existence is in place-- what Yoder calls "creative transformation."
7. It means that those at the superordinate position will accept equal status with those in subordinate position.
(John Yoder, *The Politics of Jesus*, pp. 162-192)

This is what we said mutuality is supposed to provide -- a situation in which social stratification, where selfish purposes and isolation are served, is broken, and a holy bonding takes place. Where the Gospel of the Kingdom is preached, it is to bring us back to where fellowship is understood as mutual love. Our challenge to submission is given in Christ (John 13:14,15), so that we can never live like those who have no humility, no trust, no hope, and no security.

The idea of submission is fascinating and, in the abusive context of the life today, it needs much consideration. Here, I have only given it preliminary consideration in order to emphasize that the mutual relationship of the believers is never demeaning but, rather, accentuates the dignity of the human person.

3. *Mutuality helps us grasp the significance of equality.*

Since we have spoken of dignity, we need to take up the concept of equality, for it is in the framework of equality and mutuality that people can speak of dignity. A few of my colleagues have been concerned that a theology of mutuality does not include equality. But where we find class structures, as we often do in the Church, and differing modes of dealing with people because of race, sex, and age, we cannot say the Bible does not provide the answers for the needs of the community. While we might argue the evident unequalness of gifts, talents, and potentials we find in the Bible, we can still say that the fundamental emphasis of the Bible is that we are equally accepted in Christ. We are cemented in the bond of a holy friendship. We are heirs of one great promise, and our spiritual privileges as Christians are constrained by one person -- Jesus Christ. As the famous passage in Galatians 3:28 notes, Jews and Gentiles, men and women, slaves and free, all share the same Gospel privileges, the same freedom, and the same status of equality in Christ. For Gilbert Bilezikian:

1. Differences of rank are irrelevant in the Church.
2. Differences of class are irrelevant in the Church.
3. Christian leadership or service based upon gender differences is an obstacle to progress in the Church.
4. Differences of race are irrelevant in the Church.

(See, *Beyond Sex Roles*, pp. 121-134.)

The conclusion is that discrimination which is based upon race, rank, class, gender, and age is against our common bonding in Christ. So, in building community which takes its lead from the incarnated Christ, we lift up the worth and dignity of every one. "Wash one another's feet" does not select those I like and leave out those I do not like, but it sees every one on the same level at which Christ would see them. All persons in the community are servants of God together.

4. *Mutuality deepens our sense of belonging.*

Equality leads us to focus on the sense of belonging to the community, for only where people feel equal do they really feel a sense of their belonging. In contemporary society where alienation and fragmentation reign, people have felt more like things possessed than like people possessing. People are social security numbers, birth dates, and cases -- not names. Even in churches we have adopted this impersonal style. When Martin Buber was debating with Martin Heidiger and other philosophers of Heideger's kind many years ago, the point he raised was that in contemporary society, people did not feel like "we's" in a community, but like "I's" in a conglomerate or "collective." Whereas the "we's" are bonded, albeit temporarily, sometimes the "I's" are never bonded, but often act from a crowd or group mentality. In the end, the crowd, or collective, submits itself to all kinds of uncriticized, irreverent, and irrelevant causes. Prime examples of crowd response, for Buber, were National Socialism and Communism (cf. *Between Man and Man*, pp. 175-177).

Today, we treat this crowd mentality as normal so that even in the Church as community, people "wander lonely as a cloud." Loneliness dominates, and it is taken for piety. The point I seek to make is that the Church as mutual community challenges this abstractness and sham of relationships, and builds on intimacy, trust, and love, so that people can experience a sense of belonging. The Church seeks to challenge that life where people "hold each other at arm's length," so that they can live, as some psychologists articulate, "intersubjectively." For J. R. Nelson, the ecumenical theologian, Christians need to test the integrity of their community by their mutuality (*Criterion for the Church*, pp. 71, 81). My point is that we cannot say "mutual love is nothing," for when division is evident in the Church, it burdens us and makes us a scandal before the world.

5. *Mutuality helps us understand the relevance of diversity.*

When we speak of belonging in the community, we must confront demonic forces which seek to make belonging mean uniformity. As Martin Buber has shown, there is a one-sided inclusion and a one-sided unity, where the other person's legitimacy is "relativized," "stigmatized," and "rejected." The other person must accept our way without our accepting his/her way, and so forth. Over against this falsehood of inclusiveness, Buber suggests that the constructive forces of mutuality-- that which is of God--will *acknowledge* the contributions of the other through genuine "give and take," genuine "conversation," and genuine "friendship." This, for Buber, is dialogical living (*Between Man and Man*, pp. 96-101).

The sense of belonging by which we are called to live challenges contemporary relationships in which people categorize, schematize, and label everyone and then proceed to "exclude" them instead of "including them." When each person with whom we live must fit a class, a race, an ethnic group, a sex, or some other category--real or imagined--before they are called human, it is 'the return to the tribe.' So, even in the midst of gender, race, and ethnic consciousness, we must let Christ speak more to us than does our gender, race, or ethnicity. Society does not make us penetrate so-called barriers to build better relationships, but in mutual community, the blood of Christ challenges us to break down walls and build bridges (cf. Carolyn Gratton, *Trusting: Theory and Practice*, p. 97). The philosophy in which "Birds of a feather flock together" while those birds who have different feathers, or little feather, are "defeathered" is alien to the community of mutuality.

This is why I am uncomfortable with any Church growth strategy which seeks to build a community on the basis of "homogeneity." If the Christian community is to succeed with its gospel to the nations, it must acknowledge difference and diversity while valuing differences of opinion, differences of standpoints, differences of race, class, gender, and age, etc. Whereas it might be easier to sustain a church budget by avoiding differences, it also creates a way to build superficial relationships (J.R. Nelson, *Criterion for the Church*, pp. 61-62).

Differences and diversity need not be destructive for those who recognize themselves as part of the extended family of disciples who also recognize the profound reality of community responsibility. Buber has said that we have community when a unit of several independent persons reach self-responsibility, when all impediments are set aside, and life with one another is established. If each is taking a part and bearing responsibility, then we have community (*Between Man and Man*, pp. 175-176).

6. *Mutuality means responsibility and accountability.*

The Bible is replete with examples of the practical effect (or the responsible engagement) of what mutuality can mean for community. However, I take 1 Corinthians 8-14, in which Paul instructs his church to be responsible and accountable for its actions.

In Chapter 8, where he instructs on the use of meats offered to idols, he points to the strong sense of responsibility that each member must assume towards another. Thus, those who are knowledgeable should take care how they treat the ignorant. Those who are strong should not be a stumbling block to the weak. Those who sense the liberty in Christ should not let such liberty destroy community unity. If an action such as eating meat offered to idols causes others to stumble, it is sinning against the members of the family and, therefore, against Christ. In Chapter 9, where Paul speaks of the freedom or rights of their apostleship, he notes that he will waive such rights in favor of the Gospel, but he calls for the respect that the apostolic office should receive and the needed financial support, so that all might receive mutual benefit. From verses 19 to 27, he speaks of the self-sacrifice and self-discipline necessary for the benefit of the gospel.

In Chapter 10, he bluntly attacks those who refuse to acknowledge mutual authority in worship. Although some persons reading this chapter might suggest a so-called "creation order," in which Christ is the head of men, and men are the head of women, closer reading focuses on the order of equality and mutuality where "man comes through woman," and "woman comes through man." The bottom line is that women and men find their limits in each other and their ultimacy in Christ.

In Chapter 11, he responds to the question of the Lord's Supper, and comments on the unworthiness of those who do not wish to participate mutually or corporately. They are under the judgement of Christ, for they "do not discern the Lord's body."

In Chapters 12-14, he follows the theme which he had picked up in Chapter 11, "the body of Christ," which is developed in many places as the church (cf. Rom. 12:5; Eph. 1:22-30; 4:4,12,16; Col. 1:18,19; 2:17; 3:15). Here, we are introduced to the elaborate discussion on spiritual gifts, their mutual source, use, and operation in worship, and we are given two examples of what is meant by mutuality by being asked to look at the

dynamic functioning of the human body, then at *love* --
which defines the limits of every relationship. His final
point is that "love never fails," never ceases to exist, and
never ceases to operate. Genuine love always calls for
responsibility and accountability.
The reality of mutuality is love--what I have called
"giving" and "taking." Sometimes, "giving" does not
always have immediate, equitable "taking," or "taking"
does not have immediate "giving." If we think in terms
of sequential processing, however, where love exists,
there is no need to calculate who gives more or takes
more.   Parker Palmer spoke well of "Teaching the
Public Life" when he said that we are called to put our
love in jeopardy so that love can be demonstrated in our
lives.   For as we are willing to lose our lives for
Christ's sake, God's love will flow through us to turn
loss into gain, defeat into victory, death into life -- for
ourselves and for others, too. To experience the gain,
the victory, and the life, we must be willing to undergo
the loss, the defeat, and the death offered to us in life
(*The Company of Strangers*, pp. 112-113).

7.   *Mutuality makes us more open to the Spirit's freedom.*

To be willing to risk oneself is to be truly free, for
it means one has moved from the realm of self-protection
to that of vulnerability. *Risking* is the dynamic in a
person's life that makes for creative expression without
the oppressive restrictions that stunt or kill the potential
for growth.   Freedom is the possibility of being oneself,
and of allowing others to be themselves.   This is the
fundamental principle behind the *Imago Dei* - the image
of God in humanity. For Reinhold Niebuhr,

There can be no principle of harmony short of
the love in which free personality is united in
freedom with other persons. But the coerced
unities of nature and the highly relative forms
of social cohesion established by historic
'laws' are inadequate as final norms of human
freedom. The only adequate norm is the
historic incarnation of perfect love which
actually transcends history, and can appear
only to be crucified (_Nature and Destiny of
Man_, vol. 1, p. 147).

Where such freedom can be enjoyed in the Church, there
is vulnerability.

8. _Mutuality is a potent means for personal community
renewal._

As a final function of mutuality, I speak of the
road to personal and community renewal, for by being
who we can be and by doing what needs to be done as
members of mutual community, we renew our being and
thus, our communities. Renewal has been one of the
cardinal themes in church growth discussions over the last
three decades. So I do not seek to give it any full
treatment here. I turn to Martin Buber, however, to
repeat the point that it is only through participation in the
existence of living beings that one discloses the meaning
in the "ground" of one's own being (_Between Man and
Man_, p. 193). Jurgen Moltmann puts it more simply:
"Where we accept one another, recognize one another,
and affirm one another, we are on firm ground" (_The
Power of the Powerless_, p. 102).

To get people to go beneath the surface of their

relationships is not very easy. I often tell about a time when I was sure I carried two biographies, maybe even three. And I was no split personality. But I became frighteningly aware of it when I worked in a certain place where I felt profound prejudice. In that place, the people around me seemed not to care, and I found--like them--I was beginning to develop a false air. I shouldn't make a judgment, but I found the lack of vulnerability most challenging. One day I began to note it, that I would give a biography to the people who did not care about my person; and to others, I would give a more open biography. Not that I was lying, but the superficiality and the masks just caused me to feel that I was. So I decided that place was not the place for me to find community. Any community which allows people to live without vulnerability is oppressive. Lack of vulnerability takes away one's true self and dulls the cutting edge of personal, religious experience -- the freedom to be honest. When people are insecure, they live with more than one biography, and that is dishonest. They live with just enough trust to out-negotiate, out-maneuver, and out-compete with everyone, and that is dangerous. But when a community does not offer opportunity for openness, it also must take responsibility for such dishonesty.

In his book, *Love*, Leonard O. Buscaglia tells how he creates freedom and honesty on a personal level. When he sits with his students, he says "Tell me about yourself; let me tell you about myself." In such contexts where dialogue begins, there is honesty. When there is trust, people will venture honestly. When people venture, they can be honest. When they are honest, they can be free. When they are free, they can enjoy the Holy Spirit's presence. When the Holy Spirit is present, there is community. What I have been seeking to do throughout this discussion is to make the point that any theory that we might hold about community cannot be tested until it is brought into practical, mutual relationships. For C. Ellis Nelson, a former professor of Ethics at Union Theological Seminary in New York, "Experience must be related to the affirmations of faith," and such experience is to be gained within the community of believers. As Nelson argues, "It is the relating of [our] experiences to God that makes the community of believers necessary." To further emphasize Nelson's ethical philosophy, I make the following outline:

1. "The fellowship of believers makes faith operational."
2. The community is necessary because the specific things for which one needs forgiveness happen in relation to other people in a continuous stream of human interaction.
3. "The church at Corinth had to reconcile both love and moral law and we have to do it in the same way -- through a believing community."
4. "Reality is displayed in conflict and argumentation" which can only be done honestly and effectively in the context of the believing community.

(*Where Faith Begins*, pp.95-120)

What I have said does not seek to idolize mutuality or community, but it seeks to sensitize us to the dynamic reality of our lives together -- our lives especially in the Community of Faith - The Ecclesia. What we understand is that the Spirit builds community and not just individuals. In recognition of the weaknesses existent in life, we know that mutuality has its limits. But in the Church we can confront such questions as,

"Can we love ourselves?"   "Can we endure ourselves?"   "Can people endure us?"   "Can we suffer with each other?"   "Can we get along with each other?" and so forth.   The fundamental ecclesiological issue is whether a church that exists on earth recognizes itself as a community gathered around Christ.

With Christ as its head the Church as a single living organism fellowships together, worships together, and works together for the upliftment of all humanity. The Church is a community in which there are no masters and slaves, but a community in which each one is a slave toward each other. Only *One* is our *Master* - even Christ. We, therefore, stress that through mutuality with Christ, we provide a counter-force which challenges the isolation, competition, and self-serving powers which occupy the world. From the Church then we turn to the world to build up communities of love, grace and hope. The words of international reggae artist Bob Marley are a quite appropriate conclusion:

> Let's get together and be alright,
> One love, one heart.
> Give thanks and praise to the Lord
> And be alright.
> (Bob Marley)

CHAPTER FIVE

WASHING DIRTY FEET:
Compassionate Witness of the Community

Things We Would Prefer Not Doing

In the first year of my ministry, I served as the assistant pastor of a large church. Within a few weeks of my appointment, I was asked by the senior pastor to accompany him to serve the Lord's Supper to some members of the church who were living in an infirmary. When we reached the infirmary, the pastor suggested that he and I should wash the feet of the male participants, while the deaconesses should wash the feet of the female participants. I went along and did as I was told, but with quite a bit of resentful feeling written on my face. It was not the first time I had gone to an infirmary, but the other times, I had not been a pastor and had carried a Bible and song book only to read scripture to the patients and pray with them. I did not touch the patients. I only told them how God loved them. This time, it was to be a very different experience. I had to touch, and very quickly, I began to look at them from head to feet. Soon, I began to notice how their feet were misshaped, ugly, and smelly. But I also began to perceive my own superficiality. I was less than enthused to participate in the action and wished I had not been asked.

However, upon completing the footwashing, I noted the great satisfaction on the faces of the men. Their reaction reversed my apprehension. It was then that I began to learn a lesson in the humble witness of Jesus.

I have told my story to challenge us to a deeper reflection on what it means when the community called church is invited to witness to the marginalized, the "ordinary people" in their "intolerable situations." Whether we go as lords and gods to them or servants is often a question. How do we develop the discipline of discipleship to show love to the world that is alien to us? How do we show hospitality to outsiders (*philonoxia* - "love the stranger")? "How do individual members in the congregation (the congregation at large) demonstrate that the Christian faith is related to human need?" "How does the church as a community make the world conscious that its worship together, its life in community is powerful and effective?" These were the critical questions we said we would ask from an earlier discussion. For it was our feeling that the community which lives mutually has a tendency to emphasize its particularity, its "inclusivity" and "exclusivity." That is, it tends to focus on its "intensive" direction so that it forgets its "extensive" direction. What I seek to articulate is that the Church as a witnessing community is to fulfill Christ's intention to establish the kingdom of God in the world. Only thus can we speak of a Church which fulfills Christ's non-discriminating service to the world. Those who understand themselves as disciples are to follow Christ and accept Christ's apostolic call to service in this way. *Discipleship* means willingness to follow the Lord, obey the Lord, imitate the Lord, and spread the love of the Lord (Lk. 5:27; Matt. 19:21; 2:14), while *apostleship* means to accept the Lord's commission to spread His love. In his book, *The Life And Teaching of Christ*, James Stewart expresses the idea that there are three stages on the road to full apostleship. The first stage is friendship, the second stage is following (which I call discipleship), and the last stage is the call to full ministry, that of complete service (which I call apostleship). All the stages fascinate us, but it is the last stage that engages us here, for our fear of the intolerable, the ordinary, the difficult situation, can drive us away from obedience to God's commission to confront the intolerable. The Mount of Transfiguration and the Upper Room are circumstances where it is nice, and safe, and glorious. Some worship services are like that, hard to leave. The fellowship of believers is also hard to break, but remaining in such circumstances is a minor part of our call to the community of God.

Dealing with Intolerable Situations

Malcolm Muggeridge, to his credit, makes a contrast between himself and Mother Theresa by noting that both of them were living in Calcutta in great comfort in the 1930's. Mother Theresa was teaching at the Lorento Convent school, while Muggeridge was working on the _Statesman_ newspaper. Both of them had to daily pass the squalor and poverty in Calcutta. But Muggeridge notes that it was Mother Theresa who found the situation intolerable and was humble enough to give up her comfort to go and live in the midst of the latter situation. Today, through the _Orders of Charity_ she founded and the many homes she established, poor and sick people all over the world are being cared for. For Muggeridge, Mother Theresa's favorite saying was that what the poor needed more than food, clothing, and shelter, though they desperately needed these too, was to be wanted. It was the outcast state that their poverty imposed upon them that was most agonizing. Muggeridge believed this was what drove her "crazy," (_Something Beautiful for God: "Mother Theresa of Calcutta,_ pp. 22-23). One can also add the same of Mother Hale who lived for many years in the Harlem section of New York City. Though the means available to her were very limited, she reached out to many parents in their sad situation and took in their drug babies ("junkie" babies) and later, she reached out in a profound way to AIDS victims. Before her death in 1992, she became popular, but her service was not based upon her popularity -- but upon her love.

The call to Christian service is sometimes a call to face repulsive and intolerable situations. It is truly a call to clean up the filth which spoils human dignity. What Dr. Raymond Sauls said to a group of graduating nurses on May 8, 1992 at Atlantic Union College, Massachusetts, needs to be said to all Christians, whether it is understood symbolically or literally:

> The work you will be called to do might not be pleasant at times. You will spend much time making beds, taking out bed pans, collecting urine and feces samples and wiping mucus. This is only part of your daily chore.

The point is that discipleship calls us to be in community with people we would normally despise (cf., Jurgen Moltmann, *The Power of the Powerless*, p. 96). As in the practice of Jesus' ministry, He mixed with and touched all kinds of people who were ritually unclean-- hemorrhaging women, lepers, and blind people--so we are called to ministries that are challenging, intolerable, and demanding. It is interesting that such situations are not just to be found *outside* the Church but even *in* the Church, insomuch so that we are asked whether we will discriminate. Lewis B. Semedes tells his own story of his call and ordination to the ministry, and his perception of the people he was called to serve. He notes that his ministry would have been damaged if he had not gone through terrible frustration and received the good advice from his friend and former seminary professor. Then he says,

> After some years in the ministry, I learned that a lot of people who were looking to God for help through me were ordinary people in the sense that they were living, not on the peak of success, but at the edge of failure; not on the pinnacle of triumph but at the precipice of despair. Many of them felt like failures sometime in their lives. Many were so hurt, burnt, and put down that they pressed their anger into knots too tight to be untied, and kept the door of their lives closed. Their sense of life was that of helplessness, sinfulness, and despair" (see, "Preaching to Ordinary People," _Leadership_, Fall 1983, pp. 114-119).

Listening to those who suffer, suffering with those who suffer, being with people who live out there on the edge of suffering can be quite challenging. This is why I find it necessary to call for courage as a first issue in speaking of the living witness of the community (cf., Cecil Williams, with Rebecca Laird, _No Hiding Place_; Ronald H. Stone (ed.), _Liberation and Change_). Often enough, when the community is called, it is dogged with fear. As Jurgen Moltmann said it, "Suffering, guilt, fear and grief destroy--because they isolate us" (_The Power of the Powerless_, p.108).

Dealing with "Intolerable People"

A great part of the call to witness is the call to enemy territory. The people Lewis Semedes described above were people in his congregation. The people who confront us with intolerable conditions are people we meet outside our churches. I call them the intolerable because they are not the kind of people with whom church people like to deal. They are the ones who curse at us, swear at us, spit at us, and even reject us. In Jesus' world, they were the Samaritans, the Romans, the tax collectors, the prostitutes, and even the lepers. In our world, they are the Jews, the Muslims, the Hindus, the Buddhists, the AIDS victims, the drug addicts, the alcoholics, and the convicts of every type. They are the very kinds some evangelists do not speak about when they baptize them. I have heard quite a few evangelists say, "I baptized a millionaire," but I rarely hear any say "I baptized one AIDS patient, two prostitutes, three drug addicts, and six convicts." This is not to say that witnessing to and winning a millionaire and other "good people" is not important for a church budget. Besides contributing to its "budget," the "good" people might also contribute to mutuality and share their material goods and their personal, spiritual gifts.

But the perspective that footwashing places on the proclamation of the gospel and community building impacts us with the kind of people with whom we do not want to deal. When it calls for a witness which is proclamative and active, which is concerned with preaching, teaching, and social ministry, one that takes us to the margins, it means that we must meet the enemy and the unworthy. When witnessing is seen in relation to or from the perspective of the people with who we like to work, it is quite different than when we speak of it as crossing our cultural and class boundaries. It is also quite challenging when discussed from the viewpoint of the people who are on the opposite side. Theoretically, we are supposed to know this, but when we become middle or upper class churches, which much of American Christianity is these days, we tend to have a high, upper-middle class perspective of sharing the Gospel. So we get locked up in our churches and we cater to certain classes, while ordinary people are left to eat of "the crumbs that fall from the master's table." The parable told by Jesus of the friend who knocked at midnight is not to be interpreted just as a call for persistence in prayer. Instead, it focusses on the Church in its missions today. Martin Luther King, Jr., for example, interprets it in his book _Strength to Love_, to say that many churches are dead asleep with their members inside, while despairing, hopeless, powerless people are knocking on the door outside. For Martin Luther King, Jr., if the church will take itself seriously as a "prophetic" community in its proclamation and action, if it will proclaim God's Son, Jesus Christ, to be the hope of humankind in all their complex personal and social problems, if the Church will help people deal with their nagging guilt resulting from their wanderings in the midnight of ethical relativism and their surrender to the doctrine of self-expression, "then people far and near will know the Church as a great fellowship of love that provides light and bread for lonely travelers at midnight" (_Strength to Love_, Chapter IV).

One church which I was asked to pastor was in brokenness before I got there. That is because some of the members wanted the church to move to a new area. The reason some members argued was the drug addicts, prostitutes, and welfare people in the environs of the present location. "We just cannot stay; it is too dangerous," they said. When I became the pastor, it took much cajoling to convince the members to stay, especially since those who wanted to leave were quite influential. I had to state clearly that I have nothing against working to save opulent and middle class people, but two things needed to be kept in mind: (1) That the love of Christ is "a caring love" which needs to be shared without discrimination with those who are on the margins of life; and (2) That the understanding of that caring love keeps us honest about wholeness in our strategy for sharing the gospel.

Before elaborating on the two points, I should also express that a church which is true to its character of discipleship is to confront a world sunken in moral hopelessness. To reach people and make them feel worthy in Jesus Christ is the purpose of a community of grace. "'The lame man at the gate beautiful' is a contradiction," I said. 'Pharisaic blindness,' intolerance, pious exclusivism, and self-seeking are also a contradiction to churchly mission which seeks that the grace of God be directed to the world. For while the very opulent and good people need Jesus, the people on the margins need Jesus as well. To be a community that can only deal with the "decent" people is also a contradiction to grace. Markus Barth states it well in his commentary on Ephesians that what the Church owes God is public witness, that is, witness *in* the world, *before* the world, and *for* the benefit of the world. "Public witness," he says, happens when the Church "bursts" out of its "private service" into its "public life." And while the Church is not expected to save the world, nor bear its sins, it bears testimony to the salvation of Christ when it loves the outsider (cf., Rom. 1:16; Eph. 2:5-10). The benefits of grace given to the Church are not for its private enjoyment and pursuit of clouds, but for the Gospel of Peace. Here, Barth notes that Christians need not worry about their own salvation and edification, nor of their number, for the Church that spends itself in the work of Christ is precious in God's eyes and will receive what it needs. By losing its life, it will find it. By giving itself in hospitable service, it will grow in grace and numbers (*The Broken Wall*, pp. 193-202).

A potent example of a church which moves forward with this kind of witness is Reverend Cecil William's Glide Memorial Church in San Francisco, California. Without relating the story, which is detailed in his book *No Hiding Place,* I only note that the church is doing much for people of all classes who feel bankrupt - morally, spiritually, mentally, and emotionally. The program is called "Recovery" because it seeks to rebuild the lives of people who have faced the ravages of crack abuse, sexual abuse, unemployment, and other forms of violence, as well. And it is powerful because it does not only use humanistic means to deal with people's problems, but it believes that the freedom and empowering of human lives will only come when they are also willing to bathe in "the river of the Spirit." In commenting on the church in which he grew up, Williams says that those who described themselves as Spirit-filled seemed to have been elevated out of their bodies somehow. "They were holier than life, better, above the rest of the community. 'Getting the Spirit' seemed more like an escape from loving, from risk, from commitment to real people in the world." Then he rebuts, "That's not what it means to be Spiritual. The Spirit comes to make us free and fully alive. Any church that teaches that the Spirit makes us dull, dead, at rest, removed from the pains and struggles of life isn't talking about the True Spirit. The Spirit lifts us, but not out of the earth or out of community" (*No Hiding Place*, p. 408).

The Church's Holistic Witness

In no way can it be expected that every church will replicate the Glide Memorial Church. However, the church can share its love and develop its public witness along the path of proclamation and action which I stated above. This is the (w)holistic witness of the Church as community. By "(w)holistic" witness, I mean the witness which emphasizes preaching, teaching, discipleship-making, fellowship, service and justice work (cf., Donald G. Bloesch, *Freedom for Obedience*, p. 153). Such broader focus gives us the option to start where the demands may appear. Each person brings some gift to the church, and each person will only be useful as his/her gift is used in the witness of the Gospel. So it cannot be that the Church will seek to develop a unidimensional witness if it will bless the differently gifted and the various needs of the world. The first aspect of witness which takes in preaching, teaching, discipleship-making and fellowship of the "called" must be carried forward clearly, decisively, and without discrimination. As Donald Bloesch says it, "Evangelism is the privilege God gives to all Christians -- sharing the story of God's love with our neighbor for whom Christ died. It is the peculiar responsibility of those who are called to the public ministry of the Word - pastors, teachers, and elders. Not all sermons will be evangelistic, but the evangel or saving message of the Cross should be the heart of every sermon." Bloesch carefully develops this aspect of the witness when he states that the highest service the church can give to the world is to work for the conversion of souls (1 Cor. 9:19; Jude 23: James 5:19,20). In his view, conversions take place when the gospel is preached, when faith is built, and when people are committed to the body of Christ through baptism (*Freedom for Obedience*, pp. 154-155).

One might have some disquieting feelings with Bloesch's detailed strategy for "going after the soul" however, for he sees it as more important than helping the person. What he expresses is the common tension felt in certain Christian theologies where conversion takes precedence over Christian service or where the soul is separated from the body. Such a model of witness cannot be corroborated with the witness of Christ. The salvation of the soul is not a concept to be divided between soul winning and Christian service, the Spirit and the body. Such divisions are artificial. Bloesch is correct in saying that Christian service differs from humanitarian work by virtue of its motivation and goal. For while the Christian is motivated by the love that descends into the depths of human depravity, the humanitarian is motivated only by the hope of reclaiming people for meaningful roles in society. While the Christian is intent above all on bringing people into a right relationship with God, humanitarian mission seeks to instill a sense of self-worth and social grace for this world (_Freedom for Obedience_, p. 156). Bloesch makes his argument because he is uncomfortable with certain formulations of the gospel which are social, liberal, political, and ethical. He recognizes the difficulty of his attack since he states that:

> In fulfilling the great commission of our Lord, we should avoid both the spiritualization of the gospel... and its politicization... As the Church confronts the social and moral issues of the day it must strive to preach the whole counsel of God, and therefore a gospel that will have political relevance. But the message itself should be centered on God's gracious act of reconciliation in Jesus Christ, whereby the sin and guilt of the world are taken away for all those who repent and believe (_Freedom for Obedience_, p. 85).

But one can say, even if Bloesch corrects himself, that many church members do not seek this correction for themselves. Instead, they see the activity of witness from a single side. My point is that every church needs to struggle with its witness until it ascertains that it is putting forward a clear proclamation and practice of truth. C. Ellis Nelson said it this way, "Congregation members must ... know the human situation in which they live and to which they want to address their attention" (_Where Faith Begins,_ p. 119).

In essence, the task of witness is to do so wholly. The vital thing is to understand where people are, and to begin there. In his book, _Facing the Unbeliever_, Maurice Bellet focusses on how to deal with those who have fallen away from the church, but I believe his advice is germane to the kind of discussion we are presenting here. He advises that it is best to try to understand people in their situations and not to reduce their lives to what our view of reality is. Often, our attitude can become a problem because we wish to see things our own way rather than the way they really are. The charity of many persons is affected by the dualistic view of life which is so typical of modern times. The grand divide is spiritual and material, and those who focus on the spiritual try to bring to souls their true good which is God. But the real correlation between the spiritual and the material becomes vague and equivocal. The end is a purely human and imprecise moral support which accompanies either material or spiritual help. Thus, one should not seek to formulate a language to sustain any unwillingness to take on total witness, for our work is total in its scope (p.72).

Developing Needed Witnessing Skills

With a clear knowledge of the human situation and a knowledge of what is needed in witnessing, every church should know what kind of witnessing skills to develop in its membership. The ability to be effective in working for human salvation depends upon the seriousness with which the whole human situation is taken. If it is seen partially, it will be dealt with partially. If it is seen wholly, it will be dealt with wholly. Thus, to help us build up the capacity for a holistic witness, I mention at least four needed skills. The list is quite limited, but it gives a reasonably broad range for a more comprehensive manner of witnessing.

1.   The first skill I name is **"Incarnational Understanding"**: The ability to discern from within a situation what Christ will mean for that situation. Psychologists call this "the lived world of the other," for it demands getting physically into a situation to learn how to deal with it. To use my footwashing model, I note that bending down to wash the other's feet is the road to this total understanding.   As part of understanding I name compassion, the skill to share pain, accept hostility, disillusionment, and the dialogue of silence.   Soren Kierkegaard has portrayed compassion as the challenge to the complacency of those who would be Christians.   With compassion, one avoids looking down on others as to be pitied from a comfortable distance. For Reverend Cecil Williams of the Glide Memorial Church, to whom I referred earlier, "Our God is a God of compassion."   This understanding will make "church folks" sit with those who suffer, and give love to those who have no love (_No Hiding Place,_ pp. 212-213). Only compassion (the grace of God) helps the church to have mercy. Compassion frees it from its pretense and superiority, and reveals its sensitivity, respect, and belief that some good will come out of the most intolerable situation.

2.   Another skill needed for effective witnessing is **humility**. Humility is an attitude and a skill, and it is the unspoken thesis in our total discussion.   At each stage, I give it brief repetition since it helps community to deal with marginality. For Dietrich Bonhoeffer states that, "He who would learn to serve must first learn humility" (_Life Together,_ p. 95).   For Ralph Martin, "Humility is a Christian grace.....which must characterize God's people in the outside world and in the Church" (_New Testament Foundations,_ p. 347).   Since I have constantly focussed on humility, I only mention its significance here by saying that it is basic to our willingness to be hospitable in service.

3.   The third skill, therefore, is **hospitality**.   And as we noted, hospitality (*philonoxia*) means "love of the stranger." For Parker Palmer, not only does hospitality afford us a fuller look at the outer world, it also gives us a deeper look at ourselves.   The stranger represents responsibilities in our own lives which we do not want to look at.   For example, we hate to attend the sick and dying because we know that someday we will become sick, and die.   We do not want to look at the hungry, the naked, and the homeless, because we fear we may fall into these calamities ourselves.   We do not want to confront the prisoner because we know our own crimes.   We avoid the stranger because he or she reminds us of our precarious place on earth.   But we must remember to be hospitable for we ourselves are strangers to ourselves and strangers to each other (see *A Company of Strangers*, p. 66).

To be hospitable we need to invite strangers into our private space, whether that be the space of our own churches, or the space of our homes, or the space of our personal awareness (*The Company of Strangers*, p. 69).   "Let mutual love [of the brethren] continue.   Do not neglect to show hospitality to strangers, for by doing that some have entertained angels without knowing it.   Remember those who are in prison as though you were in prison with them; those who are being tormented, as though you yourselves are being tormented" (Heb. 13:1-3).

4.   As a final skill in the list I consider necessary, I name **friendship**.   It is the ability to trust and build neighborliness. In hospitality, we deal with strangers.   In friendship, we deal with neighbors.   Jesus showed the function of friendship when He said, "I do not call you servants, but friends" (John 15:15). Graham Maxwell, who has taken a new look at God by noting the significance of this text, says that friendship means "carrying love to the people" and working from a perspective

of mutual love and respect (*Servants or Friends*). The position of Church Growth Specialists is that the failure of many church witnessing programs has been that they want to win strangers instead of friends--they want to work "top down," in contexts where people perceive the church as alien to their community. To those who believe that church growth will take place through friendship, what I say is that we need to learn "How to win friends and influence people." A list of general friendship skills I have gathered from colleagues who have lived in many countries suggests the following:

- Willingness to introduce yourself to someone you might have never met before.
- Willingness to greet someone.
- Willingness to ask questions of someone.
- Willingness to answer questions about yourself.
- Willingness to listen to someone.
- Willingness to risk hostility.
- Willingness to understand and identify with the way other people live.
- Willingness to identify with people's pain and crisis (death, sickness, etc.).
- Willingness to risk being misunderstood.
- Willingness to respect people's differences, individuality, and space.
- Willingness to take time to make the relationship develop.
- Willingness to be a bridge/link between people (of common interests).
- Willingness to be honest with yourself and others.

I will dare to make the point that it is easier to be superficial in hospitality than in friendship. And since we have a superficial hospitality in our Western culture which replaces friendship, I suggest that we need to build hospitality and friendship together. Christian psychologist Karl Menninger states, "Before complete identification in friendship or love can occur, there must be some mutual understanding, and for the accomplishment of this, we must study one another as well as ourselves. To be understood, it means that some of our worst impulses as well as our best ones are recognized by our friend, who knows all about us and loves us anyway. Once this mutual understanding and identification are established, friendship merges into love" (*Love Against Hate*, p. 273). A good friend of mine said it simply, "You don't win people to Christ without friendship."

The Mission of the Christian Community

The mission of the Christian community has been stated as the proclamation of God's word and the sharing of God's gifts.   Our conclusion is that where the community lives beyond itself, it is sharing in the mission of God. In order to keep a clear perspective on balance in the community's witness or mission, I say with Jurgen Moltmann that "Mission is the all-comprehending mandate to which the whole Christian community is called. But none can touch Christ's mission whose life has not been subjected to dialogue with Christ. One cannot fulfill the mission to other people if one does not accept the mission to oneself first. When we have this experience with Christ, we can pass it on to others. "Mission," he says, "is participation in Christ's own mission - no more and no less. Jesus' mission is the reason for ours, and defines our mandate and our potentialities. So we have to continually test our aims and methods against Jesus' mission for it is His mission alone, not ours" (*The Power of the Powerless*, p. 72).

CHAPTER SIX

THE HOUSEHOLD OF GOD:
Community Within the Community

When Families Wash Feet

As a graduate student working on my dissertation, my study of the symbols of humility sparked my interest to begin experimenting with rituals, generally, and footwashing, particularly. I therefore had a communion service in which I asked husbands and wives to wash each other's feet. That service has been one of the most dynamic footwashing services I have yet celebrated in my twenty-plus years in ministry.

As I remember it, most of the couples were intensely joyful, but there were quite a few couples whom I actually had to coax to wash each other's feet. The service immediately sensitized me to a crying need in my congregation. In another week, along with my wife and two Christian Family Life counselors, I began a series of family forums, seminars, and group discussions. Sometimes we kept everyone together. At other times, we placed couples, single parents, divorced, unmarried youth, teenage girls, teenage boys, and children, according to the perceived need and interest. The aim was to build up and strengthen the families in the church, and, as a consequence, to build up the sense of community in the church. That is the church where I remember having the most exciting ministry until today.

Having grown up in a large, "stable" family myself, and having inherited the blessings of a "stable" family, along with beautiful parents-in-law, I am always profoundly pained when I see dysfunctional families -- families who experience struggles, rivalries, jealousies, abusiveness, and a lack of a spirit of forgiveness. My wife told me of a survey which was done of a class in a public school in which she taught. In one class of eighteen students surveyed on family issues, only four students lived with both their biological and/or married parents. The other fourteen lived with a single parent, "step-parents," or one of the many other interesting parental arrangements we find today. When asked, "How many of you eat with your parents at the table at least one meal per day?" only six said they did. The rest said that they just took their meals and went to their rooms. Then, when they were asked, "When do you speak to your parents?" they said, "We don't. We just scream at each other." Simple evaluation clearly illustrates that this was a tragedy for the children, and for their families as well. Such conspicuous tragedies can barely be helped in a society in which family values are being mocked by politicians and movie stars. When neither of these influential groups speak of family from moral interest but out of political interest, we have tragedy. Of course, no one should ask either of these groups to be the moral conscience of the nation, for neither seems to know *what* or *who* constitutes family. In any case, they are destroying - rather than building - family.

Cain Hope Felder, in *Troubling Biblical Waters*, has pointed out that *family* in the Bible is not always modeled on the European nuclear paradigm, but reflects a diversity which includes such traditional forms as the African households, in which the extended family - grandparents and other blood relatives - are included (pp. 150-151).   We might also note that Hispanic families today are quite distinct from our North American family types.   Hispanic families even go beyond blood relatives to include all those who are in constant and close contact with the family.   So one can speak of padres, padrinos, parentes, compadres and commadres, and a host of other relations as assimilant family.   My point is not to speak of the differences or similarities of family types, however, but to assert that whatever the family type that might bear Spiritual and social acceptability, the church should do everything to help create stability and rebuild the family.   Strong religious values are said to be mostly dependent on early and lifelong training, and on the conversion experience, therefore, the Church needs to be profoundly interested in the family as community.

The Church and Family

This is of profound importance because the Church as a community is only as effective as the communities of its families are.   House chaos has a negative impact on the church as a family.   Many of the Biblical metaphors that refer to the Church are colored by words appropriately used to describe family.   Such terms as "house of God" (Mk. 2:26; Matt. 12:14), "household of faith" (Gal. 6:10, 11), "household of God" (Eph.2:19), "bride and bridegroom" (1 Cor. 11:2; John 3:29), "marriage" (Eph. 5: 22-32), "chosen lady" (2 John 1:1), "virgin" (2 Cor. 11:2; Lam. 2:13), "children" (1 John 3:7,10, 18; 4:4; 5:2; 2 John 1:13), "brethren" (2 Cor. 7:1; 1 John 2:10-11), all seek to draw attention to the Church as extended family. In the early New Testament church, the Gospel was preached in house churches, and the Lord's Supper was celebrated in them, also (Acts 11:14; 16:15; 31,34; 1 Cor.

1:16, Phil 22).   While blood relatives are important, the Church, as the *new family*, is formed by the blood of Christ. Its effective bonding is not natural, but Spiritual, and this Spiritual bonding does not diminish the natural bonding but gives it meaning.

J. Paul Sampley, who has done extensive work on the book of Ephesians, carefully notes that when the Epistle describes the Church, it is at the same time speaking of the family (*haustafel*).

> The Ephesians epistle focuses its attention upon the church and its relationship to God through Christ. The author as master of received tradition has a variety of ways of talking about and portraying the church. He speaks of the church as children (5:1) or a family (3:15). He refers to them as household (2:21), as a house or a building (2:20-21), or even as a temple (2:21). At other times he refers to them as a body using the widespread organic terminology ... Twice the readers are referred to as children (5:1,8). The emphasis on God as Father is clearly set forward at the very opening of the epistle... (1:3), and readers are said to be sons (1:5) (*And The Two Shall Become One Flesh*, pp. 150-151).

This means for Sampley that any discussion concerning the Christian Community will inevitably include the family. As God's family, the Church provides the proper context for interpreting inheritance, the unity of believers in Christ, the election or sanctification of the church by grace, and the eschatological goal of God for His people (*And The Two Shall Become One Flesh*, pp. 51-52).   One can see why, then, when dysfunctions strike the family, the resulting impact profoundly affects the Church.

Jesus and Family

Some individuals have argued that Christ came to break up families. But such argument is a misreading of the Scriptures, for while Jesus chose the celibate life, and called people to radical discipleship which seems to set persons against their parents at times (Lk. 9:59-60; 12:52-53; 14:18-20), His intended point was that family relations were not to be thought of as "ultimate" but as "conditional" (cf. Paul Tillich, *The New Being*, p. 107). In two passages as recorded by the Gospel writers, Jesus tried to correct falsehoods about family. "Have you not read that the one who made them at the beginning made them male and female, and said, 'For this reason a man shall leave his father and mother and be joined to his wife, and the two shall become one flesh? So they are no longer two, but one flesh. Therefore what God has joined together, let no one separate'" (Matt. 19:4,6). "And do you break the commandments of God for the sake of your traditions? For God said, 'Honor your father and mother, and, whosoever speaks evil of father or mother shall surely die.' But you say that whoever tells father or mother, whatever support you might have had from me is given to God, then that person need not honor the father. So, for the sake of your tradition, you make void the word of God. You hypocrites ..." (Matt. 15:3-7). "In spite of its radicalism the Christian message does not suggest the dissolution of the family" (Paul Tillich, *The New Being*, p. 107). It is misunderstanding of the Scriptures that explains why people seek to use the authority of Jesus for the break up of family (cf., Ray Anderson and Dennis Guernsey, *On Being Family.....*, pp. 145-146).

Paul and Family

The Apostle Paul has been maligned, also, for not supporting the family.   But this, too, overlooks his most profound teachings on the sanctity of the family.   Although he used the contemporary social constructs of wives and husbands, children and parents, and slaves and masters (Eph. 5:21-69; Col. 3:18-4:1) to speak about family, yet, he insists that the reality of the kingdom must define such relationships (1 Cor. 7; Rom. 12:9; 13:8,9, 1 Cor. 5).   If we turn to ask, "In what way can one find resources for strengthening family?" Paul would answer, "Look to Christ" (1 Cor. 1:24; 2 Cor. 5:19).

Mutuality and Submission

Since one of the pressing contemporary issues in the discussion of family and Spiritual community is the question of "subjection" or "submission" found especially in the writings of Paul (I Cor. 11:3, 7-9; Eph. 5:22-6:1; Col. 3:18; Titus 2:5), it is most appropriate that we consider it as a problem for continuing investigation.   Some people who are using the term *submission* seem to forget that it involves love, affection, gentleness, humility, justice, trust, and mutual sacrifice, so, in attending to it, I hope to affirm this.   In *Games People Play*, psychologist Eric Burne has noted that, under the guise of love, people have engaged in all kinds of power broking, and the most common sphere for such brokerage is the family.

I am therefore conscious of this power play as I discuss submission. With an open attack against submission, there is a backlash.   Thus, while radical feminists on the left are arguing that mutual submission is "archaic," "oppressive," and "patriarchal," men on the right are insistent that "submission" is the paradigmatic expression for effective family functioning.

The submission game is therefore played to find an advantage for rulership. Whereas, for example, some gems of expression might be found in Clayton C. Barbeau's book, _The Head of the Family_, he sets forth in his table of contents ideas such as: father as creator, father as lover, father as Christ, father as priest, father as teacher, father as breadwinner, and father as saint, all of which challenge the integrity of familial relationships. While the ideas seem pious, they do play into the hand of those who have seen in the father image a distorted image of God. When he says a husband must struggle to awaken in his wife "that desire for dependence and submission, and work with a real skill to bring to flower her womanhood" (p. 17), he uses language that provides opportunity for domination. And when he quotes Theodore Mackin by stating that, "A husband's artistry lies partly in bringing her [his wife's] talents into play, in making her consistently more woman and wife by perfecting the girl" (pp. 17,18), he doublespeaks and breeds contempt, suspicion, cynicism, and distrust for the dignity of relationships between men and women. He also points out that "procreation means to create on behalf of": "Men are allowed to create on behalf of heaven"; "The children born to men are meant for eternal life"; and "the marriage act is the ultimate creative act of a man" (p. 19). After many other intervening expressions of the above kind, Barbeau concluded that holiness is the high purpose of wifely obedience, and that the stewardship of holiness is the responsibility of the head [the husband]. For through her submissiveness to her husband, the wife reveals all her beauty, purity, and holiness. By helping her to be the person God wants her to be, by liberating in her the personality uniquely her own -- the personality which he, and perhaps only he among men, knows and loves -- the husband is helping his wife to achieve humility (pp. 50-51).

It is of interest that, after the above statements, Barbeau can maintain that the union of man and wife does not dissolve their personal identities, since their marriage vow is not a magic formula which wipes away all that marks them as unique persons. Also, it does not replace their separate personalities with the neuter, "we," since neither the husband's nor the wife's personality is offered to either. The "we," he says, must be created out of the one for each other. The man and the woman must both work together to create this "we" (pp. 15, 16). So Barbeau mixes a few laudable ideas to show his awareness of the human person. In any case, this mixture does not atone for his distortion of submission, as he makes the man the definer and the woman the accepter of familial relationship. There is every evidence that a pious historical tradition is weighing upon Barbeau so that he follows notables like Tertullian and Augustine who argued that the male is the perfect *imago dei*, while the female is "defective," "inferior," and "weak," and therefore ought to submit to her man (cf., Ann Loades' (editor) analysis in *Feminist Theology; A Reader*, pp. 136-148). The same phenomenon found in Barbeau appears in *Man of Steel and Velvet* (p. 257), by Aubrey Andelin. While he tries to correct the error of some dominating males, he concludes that "the most important things that women want" are:

1. To be loved and cherished.
2. A master to rule over them.
3. A voice in matters which concern them.
4. Sympathy when they suffer.
5. Appreciation.
6. A feeling that their domestic work is important work.
7. Personal freedoms: time to do things; right to go places.

In the history of the discussion on submission, there are those who have even intended to develop complementary relationships while using the social and cultural constructs to encourage control, status, and power. A fundamental social flaw which we must constantly seek to critique today is the *submission of subservience* or *submission of dependency* which is too often expected of women by men. Dorothee Soelle said it well, that "Christ did not preach submission and resignation to the exploited" (*Choosing Life*, p. 56). Here I must add that neither did Paul nor any other apostle wish for family to be the context of slavery for either women, men, or children.

Marriage and Mutuality

In speaking of mutual submission and family, I have shown particular sympathy for marriage, not because I idolize it above every other form of family relation, but because, as Ray Anderson and Dennis Guernsey say, "Marriage is ... [a] sign of the covenant and the election of God that forms the paradigm for family" (*On Being Family.....*, p. 145).

I shall critique marriage when it functions as a social contract, or as an ethical solution for sexuality, as it often does in a consumerist culture. However, for now, I point to marriage as the original, divinely-created social unit and the paradigm for understanding the impact of a mutually submissive relationship. It is the giving and taking and the mutual loving on which successful marriages are built that makes it an ideal paradigm.

In one minister's manual the suggested counsel for those getting married reads:

> You are entering a school from which you are never in this life to be graduated. It will call for

patience and kindness. Do not try to compel each other's love. Be kind in speech and gentle in action. Watch well your words. Allow no sharpness to come into your voice. Be kind, patient, forebearing. Keep in mind that words of kindness, looks of sympathy, expressions of appreciation, will be constant tokens of your mutual affection..... In the marriage relationship founded on mutual love and respect, neither should try to dominate the other. Neither husband nor wife is to make a plea for rulership. The husband is to cherish his wife as Christ cherished the church, and the wife is to respect and love her husband. Marriage is intended to weld two hearts in eternal bonds. Nothing is to be permitted to come between the two. When you are married, you take a vow that your companion will be the nearest, the dearest, and the best person of all to you. Marriage is walking through life with each other, sharing sorrow and happiness, disappointment and hope, toil and sweet rest. So, as you take Christ as your guide, you are made patient in tribulation, constant in prayer, and manifest true love and respect one for the other, your home will become a little kingdom where the wife is queen, the husband is king, and God is over all (*Manual for Ministers*, The General Conference of Seventh Day Adventists, pp. 103-104).

From his reading of Ephesians, J. Paul Sampley has noted that understanding of mutual submission must take cognizance of the social world of the New Testament and Paul's direct reference to Christ. "Be subject to one another out of reverence for Christ (*en phobeo christuo*)." This, for

Sampley, is the touchstone of mutuality and submission (*And Two Shall Become One Flesh*, pp. 116-120), and I add that this transforms marriage and makes it what it ought to be.

Mutuality with Christ in the Family

I do not speak only of marriage as that which defines family, for families are made up of many interconnections. In the Church as family, the household is large, so our reflection must continue to focus on relationships between parents and children, wives and husbands, parents and grandparents, sisters and brothers, and singles, alike. Every type of crime perpetrated against family (children, senior citizens, women, and men) needs to be criticized as unhealthy for the family. Actions and conditions such as battering women, sexual promiscuity and rape, pornography, homosexuality, child molestation, and every dehumanizing practice affecting the family, are to be shown as demonic. Those engaging in such practices are somehow to be asked to confront themselves and be called to accept the transforming life offered in Christ. Cain Hope Felder would say, let them "Listen to the blood of Christ" (*Troubling Biblical Waters*, pp. 161-166).

We should not expect to convert everyone, but church people can build their households as models of grace in the larger human community. The blood of Jesus Christ cleanses us from the world's practices and redefines what it means to be members in the covenant household -- the Household of God. Those who seek membership in such a household must understand the significance of Christ's blood for sinners. Christ creates the transformation of their spirit, and this means new households for the church.

When Dorothee Soelle discusses the impact of "consumerism" on contemporary culture, she says, "Christ restores the insulted dignity of men and women and makes them again capable of action and suffering" (*Choosing Life*, p. 65). By speaking of consumerism, Soelle has found the demon which is not only destructive to society at large, but which is also eating at the fiber of the households in the Church. *Consumerism* in its original French usage had a rather negative connotation. Today's advertisers have tried to give it some positive imaging. In any case, consumerism still seeks to get us to buy products we do not want or need, still seeks to give us false hopes of happiness, makes us seek to "keep up with the Joneses," and seeks to destroy our self-worth if we cannot wear certain things. Jordache Jeans, Cabbage Patch and Barbie dolls were all geared to satisfy the consumerist mentality, and the impact on the family has been greed, hatred, violence, and brokenness. Consumerism has made an almost complete destruction of the language of love in which we communicate with one another, and our lives, mostly utilitarian.

I need not make further commentary on consumerism here but to note that marriages, family rituals, anniversaries, birthdays, and holidays are suffering from consumerism so profoundly that the Church must be called to assist the family in staving off the destruction. In a Toronto newspaper a few years ago, an advertisement read, "What to wear to your divorce." "Sheer mockery!" I said. My point was that if our families are going to survive, we cannot allow ourselves to be dictated to by false ideologies built up by persons whose self interests make them abuse our failure for their commercial advantage. Instead, we must declare our unconditional freedom from their materialistic things and ideologies which have no real value for us. In humility and love, we must struggle to find our freedom to build family.

Households of Freedom

Using all of the positive instruction above, I conclude with Letty Russell that the Church as the Household of God must -- in itself and for its families -- seek to create "households of freedom." "Households happen where mutual love, care, and trust happen. They are not mass produced, they are not prefab 'holds'" (*Feminist Theology: A Reader*, pp. 225-238).

To build these households, we must give up coercive strategies and return to mutuality from which we can build up our Spiritual identity. In the spirit of mutuality, there is place for uncalculated reciprocity, for sacrificial love, and compromise. The point here is to build up households that are filled with the freedom of forgiveness and healing. I found a small map in Russ and Sandie Chandler's book, *Your Family, Frenzy or Fun: Creative Family Togetherness*, published in 1977, which can help us to get a quick review of those strategies that make for Spiritual mutuality at the level of family as I wish to portray it. I have added Christ at the center of the map and a few of the descriptive signs as they developed in this discussion to emphasize the point that our households are to be God's household. The general plan is credited to the Chandlers, but I believe they would accept my explicit addition of Christ, which they suggested implicitly, since it is Christ Who creates true mutuality.

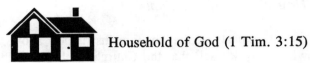 Household of God (1 Tim. 3:15)

Trust--------- ---------Openness and Honesty

Forgiveness----- ---------Kindness

Loyalty--------- ---------Concern for one Another

Integrity----------- ---------Proper Use of Authority

Spontaneity------- ---------Empathy

Love-------- --------Spiritual Commitment

Affection------- --------Support

Courage---------- ---------Friendliness

Responsibility------ --------Shared Work Load

Fun-------- --------Strength of Character

Communication------ ---------Self-Sacrifice

Thank You-------- --------Compassion

Freedom--------- ---------Equality

Household of Faith (Gal. 6:10)

I have wrestled with the issues of the contemporary family in this way in order to show that the difficulties facing the family are most challenging for the Household of God. It is my conviction that in God's house men must respect women, and women must respect men, parents must respect children, and children must respect parents, brothers must respect sisters, and sisters must respect brothers. Everyone in the family must respect each other.

One psalmist says, "Unless the Lord constructs the house, they labor in vain who build it" (Ps.127:1). So we must appropriate the guarantee of The Master Designer, Architect, Contractor, and Builder. The One who created the family will see to it that the Household of God survives as a Household of Love.

CHAPTER SEVEN

BEYOND RESENTFULNESS:
Forgiveness and Acceptance in the Community

Forgiveness and Community

The concept of community building which I have been pursuing in previous discussions is closely linked to the concept of "forgiveness" which I will present in the following discussion. It is my understanding that without forgiveness there is no possibility for community. This observation is articulated in the Sermon on the Mount and demonstrated in the footwashing, and in many other points of Jesus' teachings. And it has also received critical emphasis in our time through Dr. Martin Luther King, Jr.'s theory of love as "nonviolence." The fundamental issue is that Jesus' teachings state the tragedy of the human situation, its disharmony and disfunction, and He notes that the only hope for harmony is forgiveness and justification before God. As a good example, Jesus forgave a traitor, and at the Cross He said, (vicariously), "Father, forgive them, for they do not know what they are doing" (Luke 23:34). Thus, Jesus showed that the attitude which must be adopted for dealing with enmity and resentment within the community is forgiveness.

When we join a Church through the rite of baptism, we acknowledge that we are initiated into a community of forgiveness. That is, we accept a different interpretation of life than the world does. As Paul states it in Romans, "Therefore we have been buried with Him by baptism into death, so that just as Christ was raised from the dead, so by the glory of the Father, we too might walk in newness of life" (cf., 2 Cor. 5:14). This "new life" is the life of forgiveness. It is God's action to save humanity and promote harmony by this forgiving community. For Collin Brown, forgiveness includes discounting sins which have been committed (Mark 2:5; John 8:15), the acceptance of sinners (Luke 15:15ff; Col. 1:13), and deliverance from the dominion of the powers of evil and transference to the Kingdom of Christ. This process is stated as beginning "the new life with its promise of eternal love and life" (Luke 23:43; Matt. 5:43-48; John 14:19b). The dynamics of the process is as Brown shows it in the following simple pathway:

> --> Baptism --> Blood (cleansing) --> Conversion --> Cross --> Grace --> Judgment --> Reconciliation --> Redemption --> Sacrifice --> Sin --> Slave, ---> Servant, --> Son (Child of God). (Collin Brown, gen.ed., *The New International Dictionary of New Testament Theology*, vol. 3, pp. 697-703).

In the process, the Church's task is that of proclaiming the forgiveness which has been brought about by Christ Jesus. The Church remains faithful to its task only when it recognizes its power to forgive and live in obedience to Christ (cf., Matt. 18:18; 16:19; John 20:23).

The Extensiveness of Forgiveness

"Forgiveness" (*aphēmi/charizomai*) is an idea which Jesus often used (Matt.6:12,14,15; 9:5,6; Mark 11:26). And it is not a simple theoretical concept, but a pragmatic necessity for the survival of the divine-human community. That is, it bestows the favor of grace (*charis*), and it breaks down walls of hostility and separation. This is why I say that what is referred to as justification of the sinner in the Bible (Mark 1:4; Matt. 9:1-8; Luke 5:12-28) has creative power. Karl Barth says that the divine pardon which has taken place in Jesus Christ has a "binding force" (*Church Dogmatics*, IV:1, p. 570). This goes beyond all the mundane logic of dealing with enemies. In the mundane framework, all the logic known by humans is revenge, retaliation, and punishment. In Jesus' logic, the reverse is true. He forgives the enemy with the words of love, "You are forgiven; go and sin no more." Through this forgiveness, Christ has shown most dramatically that He can create a new way to God. In this we say that forgiveness is a miracle of God.

Forgiveness from the Godward Side

For H. D. McDonald, punishment, not forgiveness, appears to be the inevitable in the divine order when we violate its laws (*Forgiveness and Atonement*, p. 17). For Martin Luther King, Jr., "Nature does not and cannot forgive" (*Strength to Love*, p. 41). In any case, both McDonald and King, Jr. have argued that on the Cross of Christ, God passed beyond the logic of nature's laws and responded to the sinner with divine love, which meant full acceptance of the sinner. For Emil Brunner, while forgiveness is the very opposite of anything which can be taken for granted, *God forgives* (see,

Mediator, pp. 445,449).

The miracle of love that God demonstrated through Christ at the Cross is *forgiveness*. Focusing on the pathos of this forgiveness, one expositor says:

> The ultimate fact of the Christian religion is that we have to deal with a God like that, and the ultimate fact about life is that when we quit dealing with it His way, it quits holding together. Not putting up with the wrong that is done us, but matching it with something that lies far and away on the other side of what we think of as "forgiveness"; striking out toward a lost world through the very floods that have gone over us, and expecting nothing else, either in God's world or in man's! (*The Interpreters Dictionary of the Bible*, vol. 8., p. 408).

I like how Karl Barth expresses that the sentence of God - passed in the divine judgement - is "divisive." It is a sentence that results in the pardon of human beings. By "divisive," Barth means that on the Cross, God rejected sin and saved the sinner.   Such rejection and salvation, or renunciation and election, are the facts of forgiveness in the Person of Christ (*Church Dogmatics* 1V:1, p. 568).   But we should not think that forgiveness is a contradiction of God. We must simply understand forgiveness as a function of God's righteousness (William Klassen, *The Forgiving Community*, p. 157). Since the righteousness of God has been mentioned, I wish to state with Paul that in social reality it incorporates enemies(Jews and Gentiles) into the divine community (Rom. 9-12; Gal. 3:25).

This reaching out by God towards the enemy helps us to describe forgiveness from the God-ward side.   From the beginning to the end of the Scriptures, the picture painted about God is that God refuses to let go! Whether one is hiding behind a tree (Gen. 3:8), living in a pig sty (Lk. 15:11-32), or acting as a traitor (Matt. 26:69-75), one can still hear the peripatetic voice:

> How can I give you up, O Ephraim?
> How can I hand you over, O Israel?
> How can I make you like Adamah?
> How can I treat you like Zeboilim?
> My heart recoils within me;
> My compassion grows warm and tender.
> I will not execute my fierce anger,
> I will not again destroy Ephraim;
> For I am God and not mortal,
> The Holy One in your midst,
> And I will not come in wrath.
> (Hosea 11:8-9)

We can speak much to those persons who say that "forgiveness is granted _on condition_ of our _repentance, confession_, and _forgiving spirit_ towards others. That has legitimacy, but God's favor is conferred prior to all that. Forgiveness is not bound to our whims and fancies. It is proffered by God. "For while we were still weak (dead in our trespasses and sins), at the right time Christ died for the ungodly," (Romans 5:6).

According to Lewis Semedes, "God offers to us two answers to our deepest anxieties: (1) He is a forgiving God who recreates our past by forgiving us, and (2) He is a promising God who controls our future by making and keeping promises. By _forgiving_ us, He changes our past. By _promising_ us, He secures our future" (see, "Forgiveness, The Power to Change the Past," _Christianity Today_, January 7, 1983, pp. 22-26). Both aspects are unconditional, for John Wesley states it thus:

The Grace or Love of God, whence cometh our salvation, is free in all, and free for all. It is free in all to whom it is given. It does not depend on any power or merit in man; no, not in any degree, neither in whole, nor in part. It does not, in any case, depend either on the good works or righteousness of the receiver: not on anything he has done, or anything he is. It does not depend on his endeavors. It does not depend on his good tempers, or good desires, or good purposes and intentions. For all these flow from the grace of God; they are the streams only, not the fountain. They are the fruits of free grace, and not the root. They are not the cause, but the effects of it. Whatever good is in man, or is done by man, God is the author and doer of it. Thus in His grace free to all, that is, in no way depending on any power or merit in man, but on God alone, who freely gave us his own son, and 'with him freely giveth us all things' (*The Works of John Wesley* Vol. 6., pp. 408-409).

Forgiveness From the Human Side

So when we want a picture of forgiveness, we can look at the God of Jesus Christ. Now to speak on a human plane, let us admit that forgiveness is not easy. People who say forgiveness is easy have never been lied about or betrayed. If you think it is easy, try forgiving a friend, a wife, a husband, a child, a parent, or a church member who has betrayed your confidence. Try forgiving a co-worker who has lied about you. Try forgiving a boss who fired you. Try forgiving a rapist who has brutalized you or your best friend.

Try forgiving a racist who has despised you.   Instinct urges you to resent the person, to 'pay back,' and play 'hard ball.' There is even a temptation to try to get rid of the person. That is why profound issues such as the challenge of racism, the memories of the holocaust, and slavery can remain forever in permanent stalemate without forgiveness.

When Peter asked, "How many times must my brother sin against me before I forgive him?"   he was not just philosophizing.   Nor was he just reciting a social norm when he asked about forgiving "until seven times." He was speaking out of his humanness of unwillingness to forgive or willingness to forgive only a little.   Jesus understood and showed that in the human situation, it was not the easiness of forgiveness which needed to be pressed, but its practical necessity when He said, "Until seventy times seven" [490 times] (Matthew 18:21-22).   He knew that it was difficult, but He also knew that the capacity for forgiveness was an offer made by God and not dependent on the resentful spirit.   Note the parable which follows the question:

> A servant owed his lord a large sum of money and could not pay.   On a day of reckoning, the lord (master) called the servant to him and asked him to settle his account.   The servant could not.   So the lord forgave the servant.   However, on the way home, the servant met a colleague who owed him a small sum. The servant asked for a settlement, but the colleague could not pay.   Then the servant who had received his lord's forgiveness oppressed his colleague, took him by the throat, choked him, and put him in jail until he could pay.   When a fellow servant found out about the injustice and reported it to the lord, the lord sent for the unmerciful servant and treated him deservingly (Matt. 18:23-35, paraphrased).

The contrasts are:

1. God is a great forgiver.
2. God does not retain files and files of our forgiven sins.
3. We humans want forgiveness but do not easily forgive.
4. We owe a great debt to God and cannot pay.
5. God does not count our sins as "big" and "small."
6. Only by forgiveness can we have freedom to live in community.

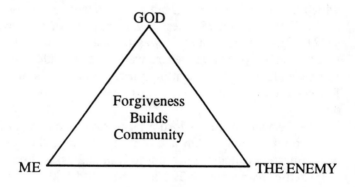

Forgiveness Builds Community

The story just recited leads us to discuss church discipline, for in the practice of discipline, we find that it is the supposed "forgiven" who are sometimes the most harsh and unforgiving. If the story can be pressed, it is the forgiven servant who is really unforgiving. Just to relate this to the church, I admit that I have seen a lot of nonforgiveness in churches. To point to Judases as sinners and community destroyers is not to help them acknowledge their wrongs. That is why I find Jesus' treatment of questions concerning the traitor quite instructive. While identifying the traitor, He used much tact, and even right down to the last day, the curious disciples did not see a finger pointing. It was Judas himself who made obvious his guilt (vv. 26-30). If discipline means to encourage the erring to confess their wrongs, seek repentance, and be restored to full fellowship with God and the community of Christ (cf. Matt. 18:15-35; 1 Cor. 5:1-13; 2 Cor. 5:11-21; John 5:13-16), then churches must work much more effectively at their methods of discipline. "Therefore confess your sins to each other, and pray for one another, so that you may be healed."   "The prayer of the righteous is powerful and effective" (James 5:16) is well understood by James to mean that a community which lives compassionately instead of judgmentally is a healing community -- and a growing community.

Since I have raised the issue of community confession, I note again that such type of communication is a real 'lost art' today. Tom Driver well states it that confession does not speak solely to the confessor but calls the community to acknowledge itself as part of the confessor's experience. "The community is legitimized as the necessary complement of the individual for every confession is aimed at dialogue.....Confession bridges the gap." For through disclosures, *personas* make themselves known to each other.   Driver finds it unfortunate that contemporary society has so split religion into private and public, personal and social, impersonal and communal, that people fear telling the truth about themselves.   In a sense, Driver feels that confession is one of the best sources for building community (*The Magic of Rituals*, p. 118-120). Deitrich Bonhoeffer believes that by failing to use the facility of community confession, we tend to live as if we are not sinners, so that many sinners become really horrified when a real sinner is discovered (cf., *Life Together*, pp. 110-111).

The point is that if we wash feet together, we may not ask, "Lord, is it I?" but will confess like the publican in the temple, "Lord, be merciful to me, a sinner." James Gustafson, taking a Pauline idea, refers to the Church and its members as *Treasures in Earthen Vessels*, for he sensed with Luther that "at the same time that we are justified, at the same time we are sinners" (*simul peccatur et simul justus; simul justus et peccatur*).

For Lewis Semedes, we are such a mixture of sinners and sinned- against, we cannot forgive people who offend us without feeling that we are being set free ourselves. Anyone who forgives can hardly tell the difference between forgiving and feeling forgiven ("Forgiveness: the Power to Change the Past," *Christianity Today*, January, 1983, pp. 22-26).

Now, since we insist that confession can and should take place in a public way, we must note that a true Christian confession begins with the acknowledgement that "Jesus is Lord." Barth said it well that the great abnormality of unbelief consists in the perversion of our relationship to Him, and that the one who believes in Him will *look* to Him, *hold* to Him, and *depend* on Him. For with the divine *no* and *yes* spoken in Jesus Christ, the root of human unbelief, the sin of human beings, is pulled out (*Church Dogmatics*, IV:1, pp. 743-746). The second point in a public confession is to acknowledge that sin creates community disruption. Some people might argue that their proud hearts, arrogant words, and evil acts are their own problems and no one elses. But the reality of community is that every sin and wrong act issues in broken relationships. Confession comes by humility, and not humiliation. So when I briefly speak here of public confession, I do not mean to ask for forced confession, but, rather, I seek to say as Barth did that the Christian is a sinful person like all others (*Church Dogmatics*, IV:1, p. 745). A free heart that knows the divine mercy will acknowledge it in turn. As the song says, "If I have wounded any soul today, If I have caused one foot to go astray, If I have walked in my own willful way, Dear Lord, forgive!" (C.M. Battersby, "An Evening Prayer," c. 1939).

To facilitate forgiveness, we do not need to add hurt to hurt or attempt to humiliate people; we only need to open ways of healing to people. It is not enough that we are inter-dependent and in relationship with one another. We must intend to maintain and sustain these relationships by being conscious of how we treat each other. Even in matters of discipline, we must make forgiveness the ultimate objective. William Klassen says of discipline that "no other mark of the Church speaks so profoundly of its capacity to love as when it forgives, for forgiveness cannot only be received, it must be mediated" (_The Forgiving Community_, p.151).

So, "How do we work with the erring?" "How can we right a wrong?" For Lewis Semedes, when we are hurt it goes deeply, and it calls for powerful resources to bring about real healing. Semedes calls "real hurts" "moral wrongs" - wrongs people do out of evil intent, and wrongs that cannot be tolerated. He notes also that we need to distinguish between the 'real hurts' and 'little annoyances.' By distinguishing between feelings which might be inflicted on us by a sour deal or by a person we love, and simple annoyances, personal defects, slights and other little things (imagined or real), we save our energy for the really tough situations which demand forgiveness. Now, I think we need to focus on the act of intent, for it was that which Judas inflicted upon Jesus. As James Stewart argues, of all the motives which have been attributed to Judas - why he betrayed Jesus, the love of money, jealousy, fear of being caught in a losing cause, desire to force Jesus' hand to declare Himself King - none is more evident than Judas' bitter, revengeful spirit, full of spite and hatred (_The Life and Teaching of Jesus Christ_, p. 190-192). And yet, amidst all that, Jesus knelt down to wash Judas' feet and to eat the Last Supper with Judas - along with the other disciples.

I believe that we should build a model from this - that even when people wish to destroy us, we will learn to forgive them, for this, too, is what makes for effective reconciliation in community. Forgiving grace makes it possible for people to pass from the 'old world order' to the 'new,' from the 'kingdom of darkness' to a 'new communal' order. "Is such an order in this world?" one might ask. I answer "yes," by pointing to people other than Christ who knew the power of Christ's love.

I think first of Dr. Martin Luther King, Jr. who called forgiveness "creative non-violence," "the gospel of love," and "an abiding faith." In the midst of a civil rights struggle which cost him his life, he taught many people that forgiveness was the alternative to revenge. With much pathos he said:

> I refuse to accept the idea that man[sic] is mere flotsam and jetsam in the river of life which surrounds him. I refuse to accept the view that mankind is tragically bound to the starless midnight of racism and war, that the bright daylight of peace and brotherhood can never become a reality. I believe that even amid today's mortar bursts and whining bullets, there is still hope for a brighter tomorrow (Stephen Oates, *Let the Trumpet Sound: The Life of Martin Luther King, Jr.*, p. 312).

I think, too, of Corrie Ten Boom who suffered through the Holocaust. While imprisoned during the years of World War II in a concentration camp in Germany, being humiliated and degraded by the Lemming guards, she stated that - by grace - she felt she had forgiven even those "friends" who guarded her shower stalls ("Forgiveness: The Power to Change the Past," *Christianity Today*, Jan. 7, 1983, pp. 22-26).

Also, I think of Richard Bernstein, a cultural reporter in

China for the _New York Times_ during the 1970s. According to his story reported in the _New York Times Magazine_ (April 16, 1989), it was through his contact with Lu Lin (an ordinary citizen in China) that he was able to publish facts on the Chinese dissident movement from a prison diary which Lu Lin had smuggled. This led to its discovery and a prison sentence for Lu Lin of more than six years. When Bernstein returned to China for a visit, he went to see Lu Lin in his prison stall because he wished to offer an apology for having encouraged the theft of the diary which led to Lu Lin's arrest.   As Bernstein went through the ritual of an apology, stating his sorrow for being careless with the document, he was shocked to find that he had already been forgiven.   Lu Lin just waved his hands and said, "Mei shi" (It is nothing), meaning "You are forgiven" (_The New York Times Magazine_, April 16, 1989, pp. 23-25, 74-76).

Those who are able to comprehend these dimensions of forgiveness can say that they understand the love which Jesus puts in place of retaliation, the reconciliation which He gives in place of brokenness, the peace which He provides in place of war, and the hope which He offers in place of disharmony. In the midst of all of life's betrayals, George McClellan reminds us that:

Christ washed the feet of Judas!
The dark and evil passions of his soul,
His secret plot, and sordidness complete,
His hate, his purposing, Christ knew the whole,
And still in love he stooped and washed his feet.

Christ washed the feet of Judas!
Yet all his lurking sin was bare to him,
His bargain with the priest, and more than this,
In Olivet, beneath the moonlight dim,
Aforehand knew and felt his treacherous kiss.

Christ washed the feet of Judas!
And so ineffable his love 'twas meet,
That pity filled his great forgiving heart,
And tenderly to wash the traitor's feet,
Who in his Lord had basely sold his part.

Christ washed the feet of Judas!
And thus a girded servant, self-abased,
Taught that no wrong this side of the gate of heaven
Was ever too great to wholly be effaced,
And though unasked, in spirit be forgiven.

And so if we have ever felt the wrong
Of trampled rights, of caste, it matters not.
What e'er the soul has felt or suffered long,
Oh, heart! This one thing should not be forgot:
Christ washed the feet of Judas.

CHAPTER EIGHT

CELEBRATING THE HOLY LIFE:
Cleansing in the Community

Cleansing in the Community

In any cultural context today to raise the question, "Should we be washing feet?" smacks of the ridiculous, because footwashing, in some ways, serves to express the sacredness of relationships among peoples. Where water is available, a person who does not want to wash is considered antisocial. The wrong odor from a foot, a sock, or a body is said to be "disgusting," "offensive," "repulsive," "nauseating," "repugnant," and something that - in the idiom - "turns one's stomach." For traditional cultures, the feet are considered the part of the body most easily contaminated and, therefore, always in need of cleansing. In contemporary culture, we generally consider ourselves clean if the whole body is washed. Thus, the concept of clean might differ from culture to culture, but each culture has paralleled the understanding that "clean" is the opposite of "dirty."

That is, in every culture people admit that dirt and defilement negatively affect community and are thereby determinative of relationships. Thus, Roland Barthes says it well that dirt - as is seen by most of us humans - is "the diminutive enemy." It is "shunned" and "takes to its heels" from out of the immaculate linen at the sole threat or judgment of a good detergent (cf. Roland Barthes, *Mythologies*). Without removal, dirt causes death. So to wash feet, hands, body, or clothes is to seek to get rid of dirt. In the United States we use *Old Dutch, Fab, Tide, Bright, Bold, ABC, Dynamo*, or any one of twenty-six brands of detergents which we add to water to get rid of the dirt. This illustrates that our consciousness of clean is so profound that we readily admit like all other peoples that water alone is ineffective for cleansing dirt away. This fact is emphasized because the significant issue of life is that cleansing helps people to focus on the moral and spiritual needs of their lives.

Community, as we have been arguing, cannot be built without cleansing. This was Jesus' teaching to His disciples: "If I do not wash you, you have no part in me" (John 13:8); "And you are clean, though not all of you" (John 13:11); "You have already been cleansed by the word that I have spoken to you" (John 15:3). When Jesus cleansed the temple of the holy hucksters, He was insistent, "It is written, "My Father's house shall be called a house of prayer for all the nations. But you have made it a den of robbers" (Mark 11:17). Here he showed that purity was the sign of the Messianic presence (Mal. 3:1ff.).

We wash today and are very conscious about physical cleanliness for our life together, and yet we fail to grasp the profound meaning of this cleansing. As Reinhold Niebuhr showed, there is an "easy conscience of modern man," and such easy conscience or unacknowledged pride had led us to social destruction (cf. *The Nature and Destiny of Man*, Vol. 1). William James spoke of the "sick soul" and the "healthy soul" as he observed the growing problem with a society so deceptive it could not admit its sins (see, *The Varieties of Religious Experience*). Later, psychologist Karl Menninger noted the

growing conceit and wrote his book, *Whatever Became of Sin?*
Niebuhr, James, and Menninger were making the same point
in different ways, namely, that humanity had come to a time
when it had lost its conscience.

   In the sixteenth century when there was a greater
consciousness of sin and a will to call for examination of
conscience, moralist\playwright\poet William Shakespeare
had set forth a moral critique of society in *Macbeth* in which
he pointed to the effort to shift sin, guilt and blame. As
Shakespeare develops his theme he allows Lady Macbeth, who
had made herself drunk and had fallen asleep in order to forget
the crime, to descend her stairs in her sleep. Then, under her
servants' watchful eyes, she says:

> Yet, here's a spot...
> What, will these hands ne'er be clean?...
> Here's the smell of the blood still
> All the perfumes of India will not sweeten this little hand.
> Oh! Oh! Oh!

As her physician arrives and discusses her actions with
Macbeth, the physician demonstrates that he was bothered by
her callousness, so he asks:

> Will she go now to bed?...
> Foul whisperings are abroad; unnatural deeds
> Do breathe unnatural troubles; infected minds
> To their deaf pillows will discharge their secrets.

But Macbeth also moralizes the problem for he, too, asks:

> Canst thou not minister to a mind diseased,
> Pluck from the memory a rooted sorrow,
> Rase out the written troubles of the brain . . .

Then the doctor answers: "Therein the patient must minister to himself." And Macbeth expostulates: "Throw physic to the dogs; I'll none of it." And the earlier remark of the doctor now becomes intensely penetrating: "More needs she the divine than the physician." Macbeth sought to deny his own guilt, but he admits the wrong when he recites:

> What hands are here? Ha!
> They pluck out mine eyes.
> Will all great Neptune's ocean
> Wash this blood?
> No, this my hand will rather
> The multitudinous seas incarnadine,
> Making the great one red.

Every Christian should be aware of this: That one cannot live with a split, contradicting, disgusting, hateful, guilt-ridden, accusing, excusing personality and expect to find peace with God or with the people of God. John said explicitly:

> Those who claim that they have fellowship with Christ while they walk in darkness are liars and do not live by the truth (1, 1:6).

> Those who have fellowship with one another are cleansed by the blood of Jesus Christ (1, 1:7).

> Those who say they know Christ (are in fellowship with Him) while they disobey His commandments are liars and the truth does not exist in such persons (1, 2:4).

> Those who say they are in the light while hating their brothers or sisters are still in darkness (1, 2:9).

The problem, as John would have us understand it, is that those who will not acknowledge their sins and guilt have not encountered Christ as the Truth, the Spirit as Light, or the Father as Holiness. Since the power of reconciliation begins when there is cleansing and holiness, I will develop the rest of this discussion following the theme of holiness and community.

Holiness and Community

Peter too is very conscious of holiness of life and its impact on community. When he speaks, in his baptismal liturgy to the members of the churches under his charge, he calls them to become holy as God is holy (1 Pet 1:16; cf. Lev.11:14; 19:2; 20:26). He also points them in the direction into which holiness leads. One direction, he submits, is that for human beings to live as moral beings, they must acknowledge their sins and cleanse their consciences. To encounter a Holy God helps them to defy their being and status as sinners. Another direction he proposes is for those who are called of God and sanctified by the blood of Jesus Christ to live with dignity in the community of faith. The third direction suggests that since individual relationship to Christ is determinative of Christianity, then those who are called by Christ should live with high moral and ethical accountability before the world. All directions are the the testimony that members of the community have been cleansed by the Holy Spitit (1 Pet.1:16-25).

1.   *The Holiness of God*

To comment on the first direction, I note with R. E. O. White, who makes much of the rite of footwashing, that the sense of the holiness (*hagiasmos*) of God has died out of modern religion, and partly because age-old rituals of cultic cleansing are unknown to us.   Thus, whereas sacrificial worship and simple public prayer demanded of Israel "clean hands," "bodies washed with pure water," and "garments newly laundered," our worship often demands nothing.   The ritual rules were no play-acting,   for they enshrined the Spiritual command,   "Be holy for I am holy says the Lord" (*The Night He was Betrayed*, p. 39). This observation should speak to those of us who only want confirmation as a way to enter the Church and a partial baptism.

Since the latter is not the contention here, nor was it for White, I focus on the more profound reality of holiness.   For it is noted in *The Eerdmans Bible Dictionary*, by Allen C. Myers, that "holiness" lies at the heart of biblical religion and, in a sense, ties together all the other great themes of the Scriptures, because it is first and foremost the root of God's being. What God does is the outflow of God's nature. God's Spirit is holy, God's love is holy, God's law is holy, and God's Church is to be holy (p. 493).

While   Evangelical   theologian   Donald   Bloesch demonstrates certain weaknesses with regard to the ethical meaning of holiness, he correctly notes that liberal theologians have failed to address holiness effectively as they try to remove the tension between love and justice.   As he sees it, their conception of holiness has emphasized love more than justice while liberation theologians emphasize justice more than love. While for him holiness carries a dynamic between love and law, mercy and justice, and grace and judgment, he argues that these are not often held together so that one can know one's sins and fall upon the mercy of God. And he instructs that the tension experienced between love and justice is not to be abandoned if we are to live effectively in the community of the Spirit (*Freedom for Obedience*, p.97).

New Testament theologian Cain Hope Felder argues in a similar vein, but he puts great emphasis on the communal relation of holiness as justice (*dikaiosune, dike, krisis*). In his view, the New Testament points to a greater impact of justice than we like to admit. Then he proposes five kinds of justice:

a. *Reciprocal Justice* forms the criterion for fairness in relation to one's treatment of the interests, rights, and welfare of others. So when a person thinks he/she deserves mercy, compassion, and love, he/she is obliged to show the same in dealing with others.

b. *Eschatological Justice* refers to the strict reckoning of God at the end of time and does not emphasize punishment but articulates the hope of repentance and God's final reward received by doers of injustice (Matt. 5:12; 10:42; 1 Cor. 9:27; Paul 3:13,14).

c. *Compensatory Justice* leads a person to correct past or present injury for the dispossession, exploitation, or violation of the rights of others. Here, Felder argues that the New Testament community encouraged its members to practice compensatory justice and not to take their cases to the law courts for, in the end, it is God that will recompense the wrong.

d. *Commutative Justice* focuses on the voluntary disavowal of one's own rights in order to reduce the possibility of future harm. This, for Felder, is where James points to the restoration of a sinner to the community of the faithful, for justice as love "covers a multitude of sins" (James 5:20).

e. *Charismatic Distributive Justice* is summed up in the idea that each believer receives his/her "due" in accordance with the manner in which each member claims and uses assigned "spiritual gifts" (*charismata*) in relation to unity, edification, and the mission of the

Church. In spite of our sinning, God shows His mercy through the gifts given to us (*Troubling Biblical Waters*, pp. 68-76).

What Felder like Bloesch has done is brought a challenge to contemporary conceptions of love, which destroy the relationship between justice and love. A better understanding of love is to link it with justice so that it may function as the organizing principle for community. In the teachings of Jesus - and those of the prophets and apostles - there was always a connection between love and justice. Bloesch and Felder correctly make the connection. However, while Bloesch seeks to emphasize the personal sense of justice Felder emphasizes its communal sense. In various ways each has contributed to a clearer understanding of the two directions that need to be pressed today, for often enough there is a tendency toward Christian irresponsibility, based upon some false notion as to what love or justice means. In effect, both Bloesch and Felder argue that we need to challenge ourselves, so that we can take with utter seriousness our duties, our obligations, and our responsibilities before a God who has called and revealed himself to us. To seek holiness as a private thing without remaining in the reality of the world cuts us off from the ethical aspect of what holiness means. To put it differently, we can say the world gives us conscience so that we can acknowledge that our salvation by divine grace makes us bearers of grace. Bo Reicke said it right that holiness is not an attribute of humanity, nor is it something we can obtain by ourselves, but only in as much as God is holy can God's people be holy (*The Anchor Bible: The Epistles of James, Peter, and Jude*, p. 84). Our holy lives are a response to grace and the imitation of the character of the God we come to know in Jesus Christ. An *Imitato Christi* is impossible without participation in the holiness of God.

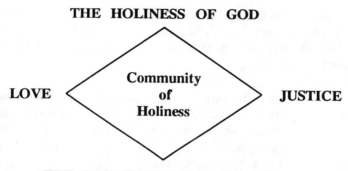

THE HOLINESS OF GOD

LOVE   Community
                    of   JUSTICE
                    Holiness

THE RIGHTEOUSNESS OF GOD

Sin is sin--both personal and social, and salvation must impact us both personally and socially. Humanity without God is unholy and unloving. So, even though we might argue that to speak of the holy life means our solitary living, yet, through love and justice, we are brought to Jesus' calling to do to others as He has done to us. John Yoder says that in these days there is so much emphasis on individualism that much fear is displayed when one raises issues concerning corporate holiness, for such fear diminishes the fact of saintly responsibility (_The Politics of Jesus_, p. 231). I have engaged in this discussion to show that there is no inconsistency between a holy life and moral-ethical responsible living.

2.   _Called To Be Saints, Not Well Adjusted Sinners_

My second approach to discussing the impact of love and justice finds its departure in corporate holiness - the call to be saints. It notes that we are called to be holy (_hagios_) through the sanctifying grace of Christ. We are called to be saints (_hagioi_), not just well adjusted sinners. The whole Bible teaches this. Thanks to Vernon C. Grounds, a _Christianity Today_ contributing editor, for presenting this idea so forcefully for our times.   In his article, "Called to be Saints, Not Well-adjusted Sinners," published in *Christianity Today*, (January, 1986), he laid out eight theses on faith and mental health that speak to this reality:

1. An individual, quite completely free from tension, anxiety, and conflict, may be only a well-adjusted sinner who is dangerously maladjusted to God; and it is infinitely better to be a neurotic saint than a healthy-minded sinner.

2. Healthy-mindedness may be a spiritual hazard that keeps an individual from turning to God precisely because he has no acute sense of his need for God.

3. Emotional illness springing ultimately--*ultimately!*--from the rift that sin has driven between Creator and creature may prove a disguised blessing, a crisis that compels an individual to face the issues of his/her divine relationship and eternal destiny.

4. Thus, in a choice between spiritual renewal and psychic recovery, Christianity unhesitatingly assigns priority to the spiritual dimension of personality.

5. Mental illness may drive a believer into a deeper faith commitment; hence, mental illness may sometimes be a gain rather than a loss.

6. Tension, conflict, and anxiety - even to the point of mental illness - may be a cross voluntarily carried in God's service.

7. No psychic healing is complete unless it is acknowledged as a gift from God *and* He is praised for it.

8. Health of mind or body is of value *only* as it is used to serve God.

What Grounds says is quite insightful and corresponds to what Jesus meant when He washed the feet of the disciples, healed the sick, and cleansed the lepers. His insight is even more profound in conjunction with Jesus' commentary to Nicodemus: "Very truly, I tell you, no one can enter the kingdom of God without being born of water and the spirit. What is born of flesh is flesh and what is born of spirit is spirit" (John 3:5, 6). To the woman at the well He said, "But those who drink of the water that I will give them will never be thirsty. The water that I will give, will become in them a spring of water gushing up to eternal life" (Jn. 4:14). In no case did Jesus ever intend that to become a saint is accomplished by physical, psychological, or moral adjustment, as the Pharisees thought. Instead, Jesus suggested complete transformation of the life, spiritual birth, repentance, regeneration, and renewal.

The above proposal is important again, and is discussed by theologians in doctrines such as justification by faith, sanctification by grace, and Christian perfection. As Jesus said simply, "By your words you will be _justified_, and by your words you will be condemned" (Matt. 12:37); _"Sanctify_ them in the truth; your word is truth" (John 17:17); and "Become _perfect_ as your Father in heaven is _perfect_" (Matt. 5:48) (_emphasis mine_). While I do not have space to detail these doctrines here, I take time to note a caution and comment made by the Reformed theologian, G. C. Berkouwer. That is, when justification and sanctification are split apart, we end up with the falsehood of perfectionism and deny the reality of the Church and of sin which -- according to the Scriptures -- still dwells in the believer (_Faith and Sanctification_, pp. 64-65).

I stress that the idea of holiness from all three perspectives is easily confusing. For example, justification, which is a restoration of the individual to a state of righteousness, is often interpreted in a legalistic way.

Sanctification, which focuses on a state of being separate and set apart, and on moral goodness is often treated as if it asks persons to live exclusively and ascetically, while practicing good works for the reception of eternal rewards. Perfection, which was intended to focus on Christian maturity, is often used to suggest that people can reach a stage of complete rightness before God through some work. The cumulative result of all the falsification of the above ideas is the notion that once one becomes a saint, such a one lives beyond the possibility of sinning. One pastor, I have been told, went to his congregation and boasted that for the last year he had lived without sinning. In the end, he was the most legalistic, moralistic and authoritarian pastor the congregation ever knew.

A correction of the falsification of ideas we have discussed above begins with what Jesus said to Peter and the other disciples: "If I do not wash you, you have no part in me." To state it in contemporary and positive terms, "If I wash you, you are clean and do have a part in Me." What Jesus does He does completely, and no work of humanity can make it up. It is not an outward or external regulation, but a complete work of God.

> If I wash your feet, your whole body is clean.
> If I speak a word (of truth) to you, you are clean.
> If you accept the baptism with which I will baptize you,
>   you are clean.
> If you are baptized by My blood, you are clean.
> (R. Kennedy)

From the personal reality of purity there is the understanding that the will of God claims the Christian completely. And the points are clear that participation in rituals of the community, such as baptism, footwashing, the Lord's Supper, or hearing the preached word, are only effective when our faith moves beyond them to the full will of

God. What is effected in us is no human work, but the will of God. We falter if through our pride we say, "Lord, you shall never wash my feet."

3. *The Holy Priesthood: The Moral and Ethical Accountability of the Saints*

The apostles well understood the above sentiments, and in most of their writings, they concluded their discussion about the call to holiness with ethical commentaries. Interestingly, Peter introduces it at the start of his epistle when he calls for holy living: "Therefore prepare your minds for action; discipline yourselves; set all your hope on the grace that Jesus Christ will bring you when he is revealed. Like obedient children, do not be conformed to the desires that you formerly had in ignorance. Instead, as He who called you is holy, be holy yourselves in all your conduct; for it is written, 'You shall be holy, for I am holy.' Now that you have purified your souls by your obedience to the truth so that you have genuine mutual love, love one another deeply from the heart" (1 Peter 1:13,14,22). In the same vein, he refers to the Church of God as the "holy priesthood" which offers spiritual sacrifices to God through Jesus Christ, a people who can "proclaim the mighty acts of Him who called you out of darkness into his marvelous light" (1 Peter 2:9).

In Romans, Paul extensively discusses holiness (justification, sanctification, and righteousness by faith), then he states, "I appeal to you, therefore, brothers (and sisters), by the mercies of God, to present your bodies as a living sacrifice, holy and acceptable to God which is your spiritual worship. Do not be conformed to this world, but be transformed by the renewing of your minds, so that you may discern what is the will of God - what is good and acceptable and perfect" (Rom.

12:1,2). Thus, holiness has its ethical and social impact, for those who are holy will be made known to the world.

I return to point out, then, that every true doctrine of holiness should lead us to Christian ethics. In one place, Karl Barth says that Romans 12 teaches us how to practice Christian ethics, for thinking about God must be encompassed by the busy world of daily occurrence which proves to us that our conversation about God is not undertaken for its own sake, but for the sake of God's will (*The Epistle to the Romans*, p. 426). In another place, he states that the fact that human action becomes the reflection--the creaturely similitude--of the divine can and must be described as the work of God's love and, also, as the work of the Holy Spirit at work in and through us. God loves humanity and gives Himself to and for humanity, therefore, it follows that humanity in their actions must imitate the love of God, responding and corresponding to it. The power of the Holy Spirit frees humanity for imitation, response, and correspondence, and makes the actions the reflection of God's own. With greater emphasis he maintains that we may distinguish but we cannot separate the Holy Spirit who edifies and sanctifies the community through the love with which God creates the community. We may distinguish but we cannot separate being a Christian from loving. We may distinguish but we cannot separate the love with which God by the Holy Spirit loves the community first, and then, Christians, and the love with which--attested by the community and its members--God has turned to all people and the whole world (*Church Dogmatics*, 1V:2, pp. 778-779).

The Ground, the Root and the Fruit of Holiness

What we have done in this discussion is to call by name the real monster which breaks community - Sin itself - as moral disorder. We have acknowledged that the solution to the problem of brokenness turns us to the ground, the root, and what Paul Tillich used to call "the Source of Being." No society and no community can thrive without a moral order and a moral voice. As we said, if we turn to the source of holiness, we will sense our sins and call for the power to build that order and use that voice. G. C. Berkouwer said, "Confession of guilt is especially common with those who know the fellowship of God" (_Faith and Sanctification_, p. 67). What we understand from this is that we are called to surrender to the divine justice. The Church should seek to live as a community that understands the moral demands of God, and that means focusing on life in a double direction. The first, as I have said it, takes one's personal sins and guilt seriously. The second is the awareness of corporate sins and disorder. The community itself and the world around it are sinful, demanding both a self-correction and a call for social order.

Thus, in conclusion, it can be said that there is no way we can cover our wrongs and live in the community without a negative impact. Again, as G. C. Berkouwer said it, "If faith will but lift its blossom to catch the sunlight of God's grace, the fruit will be holiness" (_Faith and Sanctification_, p. 193). When the gifts of Jesus are accepted in us as receivers, they evoke our confession of sin and our will to live lives of purity and love in the community of God's people!

> Called unto holiness Church of our God,
> Purchase of Jesus, redeemed of His blood;
> Called from the world and its idols to flee,
> Called from the bondage of sin to be free.
> (C. H. Morris, 1900).

CHAPTER NINE

THE WAY OF THE CROSS:
Suffering in the Community

A Parable of Suffering

In a world where chaos is being celebrated as a philosophy of life to help people deal with the unpredictability and the instability of existence, footwashing brings to us the very profound message that chaos and meaninglessness will not always prevail, but will come to an end, when through grace God brings all things into newness. From the introduction of the footwashing narrative in John 13:1-5, we get this message again, "Jesus knew that His time had come to depart out of this world and to go back to the Father, but He loved His own to the end. So, during supper, when the devil had already put it into the heart of Judas Iscariot, Simon's son, to betray Him, He rose up from supper, girded Himself with a towel, poured water into a basin, and began to wash the disciples' feet and wipe them with the towel with which He was girded." Even in the face of death He did not forsake "His disciples," and - in the same action - did not forget the world in its brokenness.

We think of the Upper Room scene again as a key to the interpretation of Christ's own life and of our own sufferings when we are engaged in the service of God, for the Christian life brings us affliction, pressure, privation, pain, persecution, and all kinds of predicaments that might lead to untimely death and the threat of meaninglessness. In the parabolic statement of Jesus, "You do not know now what I am doing, but afterward you will understand" (Jn. 13:7), Jesus meant that the footwashing was to speak profoundly of the ultimate way of pain and suffering: a way not understood. But as a drama of suffering, it spoke of the "self-giving" and "self-denial" of Christ as a Suffering Servant of the Lord. And through His obedience unto death, we are able to grasp some consolation for ourselves in times of suffering. Down to the very last, the disciples did not understand it -- and we ourselves may never understand it.

To move us from the Upper Room, we note at least three occasions when Jesus spoke explicitly of His ultimate end. The first came just after Peter's great confession: "You are the Messiah, the son of the living God.....From that time on, Jesus began to show His disciples that He must go to Jerusalem and undergo great suffering at the hands of the elders, chief priests, and scribes, and be killed, and on the third day, be raised" (Matt. 16:16,21).

On the second occasion, Jesus had just come down from the Mount of Transfiguration and found the disciples at the foot of the Mount with an epileptic whom they had tried to heal, but had failed to do so. After healing the lad and returning him to his mother, as the disciples were gathering in Galilee, He repeated to them that "The son of man is going to be betrayed into human hands and they will kill him, and on the third day he will be raised. And they were greatly distressed" (Matt. 17:22,23).

The third occasion was toward the end of His 'Kingdom' discourse, while He was on His pre-arrest trip to Jerusalem. He told the disciples: "See, we are going up to Jerusalem, and the Son of man will be handed over to the chief priests and scribes, and they will condemn him to death, and deliver him to the Gentiles to be mocked and flogged and crucified, and on the third day he will be raised" (Matt. 20:18,19). In _The Interpreters Dictionary of the Bible,_ Vol. II, it is beautifully stated that, "These three predictions are like solemn strokes of bells and warning of an impending doom. Each sounding quickens toward its crisis and climax" (p. 453). It also notes that each prediction carries its own emphasis, but the emphasis intensifies. Here, one can understand why the disciples were greatly "distressed and afraid" (cf. Matt. 17:23; Mk. 10:32-34). One can think also of how challenging it was for Jesus to speak of His own death. It was not easy for the disciples to understand, nor for Jesus to speak, but He spoke with eloquence and courage -- the high courage of lonely consecration and obedience. He also drank the Father's cup, the bitter cup of redemptive wrath and love. He then would die in utter love for all humanity. He died in voluntariness. He could have chosen life, but instead, He chose death. He could have chosen safety, but instead, He chose suffering. In the end, He cast the vote for the will of God for human salvation (_The Interpreters Dictionary of the Bible,_ Vol. II, "Matthew," pp. 464; 493).

The Suffering Servant

The key theme we are pursuing is that of "The Suffering Servant" and we shall connect this to the "Suffering Community" (Is. 53; Ps. 22:6; Mk. 9:12; Mt. 8:17; 26:66; Jn. 1:10), for those who belong to Christ's community must understand that they will share in the sufferings of Christ. The Apostle Paul declared it well when he wrote to the Colossians, "I am now rejoicing in my suffering for your sake, and in my flesh I am completing what is lacking in Christ's afflictions for the sake of His body, that is, the Church

(Col.1:24). For him, suffering along with Christ was sharing in His atonement. In Barth's comment, without the concept of "the Suffering Servant," we cannot understand the truth of the humiliation, the lowliness, and the obedience of the one true God revealed in Christ, and, in such a case, cannot understand the reconciliation of the world with God. For Barth, the concept of "The Suffering Servant" sets up "the Lordship of God" and reveals it as a quite free - but quite necessary - decision. By a "necessary decision," Barth meant that to go the way of the Servant of God was to understand the way downward, to lowliness, and finally to the Kingdom. "The Suffering Servant," as Barth sees it, activates and reveals the unconditional royal power of God by living it out unconditionally as a human being, and by the miracle of the empty tomb, attests that Jesus as a human being could pursue this way to the bitter end (*Church Dogmatics, IV:1*, pp. 157-210). The fact of the matter is that the death of Christ exposed the power of evil for what it is. For He showed that His *exousia* was only from God and such *exousia* could follow the way of humility.

For Dietrich Bonhoeffer, Christians really need to learn this humbling of power from Jesus. For they cannot shake off their sufferings as if they do not hold solidarity with Christ in suffering; they, too, have their Crosses. They are called to suffer and must be prepared to face privation, mockery, rejection, and even persecution. While they do not look for suffering, they must expect to bear the suffering which comes their way as they try to follow the Christ of the Cross (*The Cost of Discipleship*, p. 122). Not until we understand all of the above as Christians can we face both the darker side and the lighter side of life. Our identity with Christ is not only that of glory -- but also that of suffering.

Suffering and the Christian Community

In speaking of the Christian and suffering, Karl Barth reminds us that real Christians are people who suffer. They suffer because they are humans. They suffer even more because they are Christians, and as Christians, the world causes them to suffer as the witnesses of Christ. They suffer because through their witness they bring suffering upon themselves, and they suffer because their fellowship with Christ inevitably plunges them into affliction (_Church Dogmatics,_ IV:3, pp. 618-620). Thus, suffering is the reality of their existence.

It is tragic in a way that the popularity of Christianity does not allow us to identify with a suffering Christ, but with a Christ who carries swords and bombs. What is happening in Ireland and other places of the world where Protestants are in conflict with Catholics and visa versa is a contradiction of the cause of Christ. And when in the name of God and missions, Christians manipulate and oppress people, it is also a tragic misrepresentation of the suffering of Christ. What needs to be made known here is that the demonic powers which rule the world find themselves among Christians and inflict sufferings in the name of God.

In any case, it is the world that is against Christians -- for the life they lead, the law they keep, and the stand they take. To be a Christian is to suffer, for Christian witness is suffering. And it is the greatest pity of the Church when Christians fail to witness in suffering. The world has tragic situations which need attention, and the Church's involvement in them is a cause of suffering for Christians. The Church, in the sense that it understands the footwashing and crucifixion experiences, is in a fellowship of suffering. In his book _The Crucified God,_ Jurgen Moltmann, taking a lead from Karl Barth, explains in the most profound way that a call to follow Jesus is also a call to share in His suffering and to stand beneath His Cross. When Moltmann asks, "What is suffering?" he answers that it means to be rejected, for rejection takes away the dignity of suffering and makes it dishonorable suffering. To die on a Cross means to suffer and to be rejected as an outcast. If those who follow Jesus are to take their Crosses upon themselves, they must recognize that they are taking on circumstances that will not make them always happy, but many which will make them sad. The expression "cross," for Moltmann, means the suffering we undergo in serving others for Jesus. Suffering, here, takes its meaning solely from the Cross of Christ, not from natural or social causes, for the Cross of Christ was His own Cross in the service of humanity. Our suffering ought to be a service for those we are called to serve.

Lay theologian/novelist C. S. Lewis made some interesting points about the Christian and suffering in his little book *The Problem of Pain*. Here I extract the substance of four of these points which he makes explicitly, and note a fifth which he makes implicitly.

(1)   There is a paradox in the suffering of Christians, for while the Christian is called to suffer and to learn the will of God, the suffering of Christians is a temptation to disobedience.

(2)   The suffering of Christians has a redemptive element and will never cease until the world is redeemed or is not further redeemable.

(3)   The nature of the world allows God to withhold from Christians the settled happiness and the security they desire.

(4)   The Christians' suffering can be made worse if they spend all their time being overly anxious about it, as if God is not bigger than their suffering.

(5)   Suffering is incarnational for it makes us empathize

> with the pain of another and urges us to deeds of
> mercy on behalf of others.   (See Chapter 7.)

I will add that the assurance for those who suffer is that Christ
is with us in every suffering situation.

Before focusing further on the Christian community's call
to suffering, we need to remind ourselves like William Barclay
that a charge made against Christianity has been that it takes all
the light, the zest, and the joy out of life, and that some people
have seen Christianity as that which makes them do all the
things they do not want to do while abandoning all the things
they would have liked to do. A sad Christianity, as Barclay
states it, is nothing but a distortion, for Christians do live
happily here and now, and will live happily in the ages to
come. Christianity is not the choice between living unhappily
now and living happily in the great tomorrow, but the privilege
of enjoying life today, though sometimes only through the eyes
of hope (and tears) that look to life in the bliss of tomorrow
(_And Jesus Said....._, p. 152).

Suffering and Social Justice

The very idea that Christ suffers in us, suffers for us, and
calls us to suffer with Him makes the Church a community of
suffering. This is what we have been insisting upon. Not only
does the Church suffer for others or suffer with others, but it
is the blessing of the Church that it also makes suffering
bearable. This happens because, as Christians fellowship
together, they can share their pain. This sharing of pain is the
basis for healing. The history of the Black Church in America
with its volumes of slaves' songs, spirituals, blues, and gospel
songs, et cetera, may be the best contemporary example of
shared suffering in a community. I shall not make further

comment here, except to say that it is a tragedy that there are communities of Christians who are so individualistic and privatistic that they know no sharing of pain today.

In a broken society where people face divorce, sexual abuse, economic distresses, sickness and disease, and the many tragic moments of suffering consistent with our times, the Church must provide the reality of the new community. What the Church has that others do not have is Christ, and Christ gives us love, faith, and hope as the source of encouragement to those who suffer. Paul said, "We suffer so that we may be able to comfort those who are in any type of affliction, with the comfort with which we ourselves are comforted by God" (2 Cor. 1:3-11). So we might say that the world offers many hopes against suffering, such as ecstatic drug relief, yoga, psychotherapy, and all kinds of strange prospects, but the community of Christ offers faith, hope, and love.

As a practical comment on the faith, hope, and love I name, such kinds of actions as the setting up of a hospice situation in the home of a terminally sick member where other church members can take turns to serve and encourage the terminally sick one. I also mention visitation as a way of dealing with isolation among the membership of the Church. Visitation has been well understood in the history of the Church, although it is being done with less frequency in our increasingly busy times. But it needs much encouragement again since its practical effect in building up the community is so powerful.

Another way in which the Church can deal with the suffering and the hurting is through advocacy work. By advocating, I speak of working on behalf of social justice issues such as homelessness, joblessness, parentlessness, hunger, and the many other social ills which cause suffering. Advocacy means dealing with the destructive forces of teenage pregnancy, abortion, AIDS victims, and people with chemical dependency, and speaking on behalf of the disinherited of society. I have told a few of my friends that I had a great opportunity for personal experience in faith development when I tried to sell a house in New York City, and it did not sell for more than a year. When I could not find any more money to pay the mortgage and the tenant would not pay the rent, I came to the point where I made a covenant with my wife. "Darling," I said, "thank God, if the house goes, I have you." As I thought of the eight hundred thousand persons whose houses were being lost, I realized that my near loss was a gain. For now, I could begin to encourage people, since I had learned much of how to survive in a difficult economy, and I began to share survival strategies with others. The task of the Church in relieving suffering was never brought home so profoundly to me, and I say more earnestly now, we cannot just sit back and watch from the pew, but we must be compassionate by engaging in liberative actions.

Jesus was known as the Great Physician and Compassionate Savior because He had profound concern for human needs. When He sent out His disciples, His commission indicated His serious interest in relieving the suffering of the sick, the cleansing of the leper, the raising of the dead, and the will to deal with every circumstance which might help people in bondage.

The Resurrection

The Christian's life is not centered in sickness, suffering, and death, but in the hope of Christ's resurrection. The resurrection of all humanity - of the righteous and even the wicked - is the sign that God is in control of the evil powers. While we do relief work or give temporary encouragement to those who are suffering, we should not feel we have given a final answer to suffering until we have spoken of the resurrection and the parousia. An old spiritual puts it:

> I'm so glad troubles don't last always;
> I'm so glad troubles don't last always;
> I'm so glad troubles don't last always;
> Oh my Lord! Oh my Lord! What would I do?

While Katherine Mansfield could only say in her short play, "The Garden Party":

> This life is we-e-ary,
> Hope comes to die.
> A dream a-wa-kening
> (Quoted in Marvin Magalaner & Edmond Volpe,
> *Twelve Short Stories*, p. 35).

Paul could say, "Wherefore comfort one another with these words" (1 Thess. 4:17), for the faith of the Church is rooted in the resurrection of Jesus Christ. Faith in a living Jesus means that in every moment of sorrow we can declare our promise of victory over suffering. The Church repeats this to itself and to the world in its worship and witness.   As Karl Barth, whom I have quoted often, says, those whom God has called out of their temporal existence and ministry are not set into the darkness of "no more being" (death). For God takes them out of the darkness of the present 'not yet' and places them into the light of His consummating revelation. "Together with all that will only have been when He comes, their concluded existence, though it be only a torso or the fragment of a torso, will be seen as a ripe fruit of His atoning work, a perfect manifestation of the will of God fulfilled in Him" (*Church Dogmatics, IV:3*, pp. 928-929). This means that the Church can be patient for it lives with the blossoms of hope.

The fruits are often invisible, yet, the Church need not abandon hope or give up the struggle. Through its total surrender to Jesus Christ, it will realize its hope.

The Life in Hope

A story of two persons I met on one of my pastoral visits many years ago is relevant here. I tell it with some embarrassment since it reveals my predicament in a difficult situation. But beyond my embarrassment or predicament is a profound statement of life in hope. I had no personal knowledge of who I was supposed to visit, but I accepted my friend's invitation to go and see his friend in the hospital. When I went to the hospital, I was directed to the patient's room. As I entered, I began to clarify the information I had received at the desk with the first person I saw standing by the patient's bed. To my chagrin, I found I had alienated the person. As I later found out, it was the patient's daughter whom I was asking for the clarification. Evidently I had said too much. She did not wish to speak of her mother's death. In fact, once I mentioned that I was asked to visit by Mr. so-and-so (who to her knowledge was a funeral director), the daughter became angry and left the room. She emphatically did not want her mother to know that death was near.

I did not understand it all until later. But when the daughter left the room, I made my acquaintance with her mother and began to talk about the promise of Christ's second coming, the resurrection of the righteous, the need to prepare for death, and all the other great themes of hope amidst despair of which a minister speaks in a dying patient's room. I was then quite encouraged when I learned that the mother was a Christian of many years, who had a strong faith in the Second Coming and was not afraid to speak of death and the future. Unlike her daughter, she faced her contradiction of life with hope - the blessed hope. This gave her the power to resign herself to the will of God. She was not afraid to live or to die (Phil. 1:21-22).

I went to comfort her; she comforted me. Even to the very last, her words were a testimony that death is not the end, that suffering will not have power over the righteous forever. She understood it well that,

> There are trials in life
> That seem more than I can bear.
> There are heart aches beyond compare.
> Without trials in life I might never bow in prayer,
> And I would never know that Jesus really cares.
> Without trials in life you might never call on the Lord,
> And you would never know the joy of answered prayer.
> Without trials in life you might never hear the words,
> "Well done, My faithful servant.
> Come in and glory share."
> And it's the trials that bring us close to heaven.
> It's the trials that bring blessings untold,
> And it's the trials that bring us close to Jesus,
> And it's the trials that make us pure gold.
> Yes, it's the trials that make pure gold.

She understood well that the community that suffers with Jesus is the community that shares victory at the end.   As C. S. Lewis says it, "Death thins the fellowship" (cf., C. S. Lewis, *Spirits in Bondage*, "Songs of the Pilgrim," line four). But every true child of God knows that there is an unbroken fellowship -- by and by.

In a letter written to his sweetheart on Christmas Eve, 1513 A.D., a gentleman named Giovanni beautifully described how, amid the stresses and struggles of time, one can celebrate the signs of victory and keep in mind the hope of tomorrow.   I have been told that thousands throughout the world have read the letter as a means of inspiration, and that each time it is read, it receives new phrasing.   I myself have never found its true source, but I carry it on a fly leaf in my scrap book and will quote it here:

Most Noble Contessina,

I salute you.   Forgive an old man's babble. But I am your friend, and my love for you goes deep.   There is nothing I can give which you cannot take.   No heaven can come to us unless our hearts find rest in it today.   Take Heaven!   No peace lies in the future which is not hidden in this present little instant.   Take peace!   The gloom of the world is but a shadow.   Behind it, yet within our reach, is joy.   There is radiance and glory in the darkness, could we but see; and to see, we have only to look. Contessina, I beseech you to look.   Life is so generous a giver, but we, judging its gifts by their covering, cast them away as ugly or heavy or hard. Remove the covering and you will find beneath it a splendor, woven of love, by wisdom, with power. Welcome it, grasp it, and you touch the Angel's hand that brings it to you.   Everything we call a trial, a sorrow, or a duty; believe me, that Angel's hand is there; the gift is there, and the wonder of an overshadowing Presence.   Our joys too; be not content with them as joys.   They, too, conceal diviner gifts.   Life is so full of meaning and of purpose, so full of beauty--beneath its covering--that you will find earth but cloaks your heaven. Courage, then, to claim it; that is all!   But courage you have, and the knowledge that we are pilgrims

together, wending, through unknown country,
home. And so, at this Christmas time, I greet you;
not quite as the world sends greetings, but with
profound esteem, and with the prayer that for you,
now and forever, the day breaks and the shadows
flee away. I have the honor to be your servant,
though the least worthy of them.

I add to these lines words written by Dale Oldham,
Gloria and William Gaither from their song "I Believe in the
Old Rugged Cross":

I believe that this life, with its great mysteries,
Surely someday will come to an end.
But faith will conquer the darkness and death
And will lead me at last to my Friend.

Thus we can live with the air of confidence that God will
not forget us in all of our night of darkness and distress. For
even though Christ is on the way to His Father's house, He is
gone to prepare a place for those who have been cleansed by
Him.

CHAPTER TEN

PREPARATION FOR THE FEAST:
Fellowship in the Eternal Community

Sharing in the Feast of Love

We have connected footwashing with many things, and especially have we emphasized its significance for the humiliation of Christ (Phil. 2:5-8). But we conclude now with the point that it is a preparation for the eschatological feast where the community of the faithful shall sit at the table with Christ in the eternal kingdom. It is necessary to restate this for what we said of footwashing is that it helps us to view life not just in conflict but in harmony, not just in disorder but in order, not just in disunity but in community. What has been accepted as the reality of existence - pain, sorrow, brokenness, and the contractions of life - is challenged and transformed in a reality of harmony and peace. While we try to lead our lives of joy, ecstacy, and effervescence in this life of brokenness, alienation, and disaffection, we can think about the fact that we perspect about the joy, the ecstacy and the effervescence which are not only brief flashes but abundant, everlasting joy. The ones who know Christ realize that Christ knows the way out of this world to the Father's house (Jn. 13:1). They also accept with full resolve that Christ has gone to prepare a place for those who want to be with Him where He is (Jn. 14:1-3). Judas is not there to cause disharmony.

Beyond Chaos

Our reflection on community brings us to the idea of preparation to live in the Father's house. However the idea is to be interpreted, it is the way of grasping at the reality of the eternal festival celebration. Donald Bloesch would have us understand that "The Christian hope is the perfect realization of love, the perfect fellowship of believers, in the eschatological city of God." For to live in this world is to "endure tribulation and disillusionment." It is to be confronted with conflict in the face of hostile powers. But above the darkness we can focus on the fact that "Jesus is the Victor" (*Freedom for Obedience*, pp. 98-99).

To share in the privileges of the feast every Christian must take with utter seriousness Jesus' key statement to Peter, "Unless I wash you, you have no share with Me" (Jn. 13:8). This phrase is said to be confusing. For some commentators, the words of Jesus reflect *the part* we must *share* in His sufferings, while for others, it is "the heritage of Israel" or the *part* we must *share* in the Kingdom (*Basileia*) of God. As an example of the conflict of interpretations, I quote from the *Interpreter's Dictionary of the Bible*:

> [The] interpretation of *meros* [part] in John 3 is reinforced by the fact that Jesus speaks of a heritage "with Me." The theme of the union of the disciples with Jesus in heaven appears in the Last Discourse (xiv 3, xvii 24). By way of distant similarity, it is interesting that in the Lucan account of the Last Supper the question of the disciples' position in the future kingdom was raised: 'You may eat and drink at my table in the kingdom' (Lk. 22:30)...

Therefore, it is clear that the footwashing is something that makes it possible for the disciples to have eternal life with Jesus. Such emphasis is intelligible if we understand footwashing as a symbol for Jesus' salvific death...[Then] we may have here John's way of stressing the necessity of accepting the scandal of the cross (Vol.8, 1566).

But "What does the Messiah offer?" we can ask. Is it suffering or the privilege of joy? Having concluded the footwashing and the meal, Jesus knew the anxiety and the questions in the hearts of the disciples, "If this is the last meal, then what is about to happen?" And Jesus assures them: "Do not let your hearts be troubled. Believe in God, believe also in me. In my Father's house there are many dwelling places. If it were not so, would I have told you that I go to prepare a place for you? And if I go and prepare a place for you, I will come again and will take you to myself, so that where I am, there you may be also" (Jn. 14:1-3).

The news is too exciting for words, but it can be briefly stated that Jesus' proclamation of the kingdom does not end with death. Christians must protest against chaos, for chaos is not the end. The suffering, subjugation, oppression, tribulation, and persecution which are often spoken of in the Gospels and the Epistles are never shown to be ultimate goals. They only lead to character formation and inspiration for focusing on the eternal reality of joy. When the children of God sit at the table in the Kingdom of Love, they will say that the suffering has been cheap enough. John is rather insistent that those who are washed will share in the kingdom and participate in the feast (Jn. 16:33; Rev. 2:7,11,17,26; 3:5,12,21; 21:7). And Paul likewise asserts that, "Those who receive the abundance of grace and the free gift of righteousness (shall) exercise dominion in life through the gift of the one man, Jesus Christ" (Rom. 5:17). This is no "utopian" dream in a worldly sense, not a vacuum, not a day of small things, not a day of beginnings, not a time of emptiness, nor a moment of wanting, but a Day of Days, when the fulfillment of the promise shall come to life, and sorrow shall turn to joy.

In spite of the floods of life that challenge us now, the negatives of existence that defeat us, and the unfulfilled state of every living thing here, we can prepare for a feast in Glory.

Repentance as Preparation for the Feast

The novelty of the preparation is spoken of constantly in the New Testament. When Jesus said to Peter at the end of the footwashing and the Last Supper, "Where I am going, you cannot follow me now, but you will follow afterward" (Jn. 13:36), He meant to indicate that Peter needed more time for preparation. In Barth's view, the Christian's life is to be lived in the expectation of the coming of Jesus Christ to judgment, and, therefore, of the joy of eternal light. It is a step out of the present and into the future of which the outstanding event of the revelation is on the horizon, so that one cannot enter it, save in the expectation of its coming (*Church Dogmatics*, IV:3, part 2, p. 934). Such expectation, we may recite, is what calls for the preparation. To use the words of Jesus, as they are recorded by Matthew to indicate the presence of the Kingdom, "Repent, for the Kingdom of Heaven has come" (Matt. 4:17 NRSV).

This means the dominant idea that has been emphasized between the time of the expectation and the time of the consummation is *repentance*. Every Gospel writer and all the writers of the Epistles make this emphasis, and they correspond with Jesus' message. In His parables on the **parousia**, Jesus speaks of watchfulness, faithfulness, steadfastness, and devotedness, et cetera, which demand repentance -- every idea pointing to a state of preparedness.

Before the list of the five parables on the *parousia*, Matthew records the challenging parable of a guest who had gone to a king's wedding banquet without the appropriate clothing, and was deservedly condemned. Although the man had just been picked up from the streets, the king censured him, because he was offered the proper clothing but chose not to wear it, and went to the wedding "without the wedding garment." Some persons argue that he might not have understood the form of dress as the first invitees did, but the parable indicates that, somehow, he was still held responsible. For either the clothing was offered in the vestibule of the banquet hall, or it was inexpensive enough and abundantly available, so that it could be obtained on the shortest notice. Whatever explanations might be given, it is striking that, in the observation of the master of the feast, the man remains speechless. The evidence is that he understood, for no one was invited to the feast without the gift of grace which brings repentance (Matt. 22:1-14). Jesus' fundamental demand for the kingdom has been repentance (*metanoia*). Whether He says, "Go and sell all that you have and come follow me," or He gives a fully developed sermon as He does in His words from the Mount, or emphasizes it in parable after parable, the message is pointed -- "Repent, for the kingdom of heaven is very near to you!"

Matthew's four parables on the *parousia* prefaced with the mini-parable of the burglar (Matt. 24:43), therefore follow the point of repentance as preparation. Some individuals have focused on the preface to the parables with weird theories of "rapture," but the emphasis is on the contrasts of those who have repented and who will be watching and waiting for the return of their Lord, with those who fail to prepare for the meeting with their Lord. This contrast in characters is emphasized in all the parables.

Two of the parables are on the subject of stewardship. The first is in Matthew 24:45-51, while the other is in Matthew 25:14-30. In the former, the master comes and finds the faithful steward at work, while the evil steward becomes cynical, suspicious, misanthropic, pessimistic, sarcastic, scornful, bitter, and virulent. In the second parable, the servants who have wisely invested their talents are named "good and faithful" and are ready to enter into "the joy" of their master, while the unfaithful take preparation lightly, and only seek to sanctify their indifference with long excuses. The faithful are blessed while the unfaithful and self-possessed are cast away.

In the parable of the ten young ladies, only those who are awake and have oil in their lamps are ready to enter into "the marriage feast." All go to meet the bridegroom. All have lamps. All have oil. But only the wise have excess oil. At the end when the announcement of the bridegroom is made, only those who have the excess can rekindle their lamps to go in with the bridegroom. The *prepared* are contrasted with the *unprepared*. The unprepared go to buy oil, and the bridegroom comes and goes into the banquet hall. When the unprepared return to enter the banquet, they are confronted with two of the saddest comments in the parables of Jesus: (1) "The door is shut," and (2) "I know you not" (Matt. 25:1-13). Matthew appropriately ends his list of parables with judgment on the nations, for the call for preparation (repentance) is for all humanity. The key as I cite often from John 13 is, "Unless I wash you, you have no part with me."

In effect, opportunities are lost and are non-redeemable. Judas only participates in the external ritual of the footwashing, but its efficacy has not been felt. The reality is that secretly he rejects his Lord's invitation to be washed clean, and soon goes out into the night and hangs himself. The privileges given to him were not grasped. He dismissed the invitation given him and could not reclaim it.   The guests at the wedding, the servants, and the young ladies, all need to show respect and faithfulness to the One who offers forgiveness. It is not a time of passive preparation, but a time characterized by actively serving (Jn. 13:14). As the apostle Paul emphatically instructs, "Be careful how you live, not as unwise people, but as wise making the most of the time, because the days are evil" (Eph. 5:15,16). The Master, the Lord, the Bridegroom - is preparing the Kingdom. He is elaborately preparing a feast, and nothing less than careful and complete repentance is acceptable to Him (cf., William Arnot, _The Lesser Parables of Our Lord_, pp.554-581).   In a general reflection on the parables of the _parousia_, William Barclay says that the Jews believed that when the Messiah came and the new age dawned, the greatest event would be a banquet at which all the children of Abraham would sit down while the nations would be left outside. So Jesus took this idea and used it in an extremely interesting way. By comparing "the Kingdom of Heaven" to a banquet or an occasion of joy, He touched the very heart of Jewish religion, but focused the idea in a Christological direction. In the end, the Son of Man is shown coming in glory, sitting on the throne of His glory (_And Jesus Said_, p. 152). Judgment - as we might say it - comes _before_ the feast.

The Days of Preparation and the History of the Feasts of Israel

The history of the feasts of Israel can help us understand the idea of preparation very well. For as it is stated in the Levitical code, full preparation was demanded (Lev. 1-7; 11-15; 18-22) and had to precede every feast (Lev. 23). Following the Jewish calendar of months, the history of the feasts are as follows:

(1)   The Spring Festival, or the Passover, which included the Feast of Unleavened Bread (*Pesah Massothi*) was the leading festival (Exod. 12-13).

(2)   Fifty days after Passover came the Feast of Weeks (*Shavuoth*) and in the New Testament Pentecost, the Feast of First Fruits followed (Lev. 23:15-16).

(3)   The New Year Feast (*Rosh Hashanah*), or the Feast of Trumpets, came next (Lev. 23-24).

(4)   Then came the Day of Atonement (*Yom Kippur*). This festival was the feast to rededicate the temple and the nation of Israel (Lev. 16 and 23:26-32).

(5)   Then the Feast of Harvest/Booths (*Sukkoth*) came at the time of thankfulness (Lev. 23:34-36).

(6)   Later, many festivals were added, such as the Feast of Dedication (*Hanukkah*) and the Feast of Lots (*Purim*), which commemorated the revenge of the Jews against their enemies.

Each feast looked backward, but also pointed forward with great anticipation to a time of liberation from the oppressive forces of the enemies. In no case would one seek to celebrate the feast without participation in the preparation rites of holiness. According to the narrative of the Passover feast in Exodus, Deuteronomy, and Numbers, a lamb was slain by each family on the evening of the fourteenth of Nisan. The lamb's blood was then sprinkled on the lintel and the two door posts of each house to signify their preparation to face the judgment of Yahweh and a request for Yahweh's mercy and salvation. As the Passover was celebrated, the whole family ate the lamb with unleavened bread and bitter herbs as a reminder that the oppression would not last. Then, for seven days following the fourteenth of Nisan, a number of prescribed sacrifices were offered as part of an expiation system. The sixth day was "the Preparation Day," for the High Sabbath was to come. In the history of the feast, the Sabbath, too, was significant as a time of rest and peace.

For Jurgen Moltmann the Sabbath is the sign of the eschatological banquet, not only as a day of rest from work, but as a day to eat, and drink, and praise the Lord. In its history, he says, the spiritual meaning of the Sabbath goes back to the creation story, and, as such, speaks of God's goal for dealing with the world, from the creation to the last days. And it reaches forward to the "Messianic Era," for the "Messianic Era" is the "era of (_eudlem_) Sabbath." Thus, the weekly Sabbath is an anticipation and preparation for the Messianic Banquet and must be celebrated as such (_The Church in the Power of the Spirit_, p. 269).

Moltmann's comment resonates with the idea in Hebrews 4 where "the rest of God" (_katapausis_) in the earthly Canaan land and the eschatological "Sabbath rest" (_Sabbatismos_) are compared. The time in the earthly Canaan is only time to prepare for entry to the eternal rest. The symbol of Sabbath which came each week was to help the people to sense that it was time to prepare for the feast of the eternal Canaan. It was unfortunate that only few of Israel could grasp the interconnection, and thus they failed "to enter God's rest." But "there remains a rest for the people of God," a feast that cannot be described in human speech.

Another significant event in the history of the feast that was quite significant was the Day of the Atonement. The Day of Preparation that led to the Day of Atonement was marked by rest and penitence. On this day the High Priest sacrificed a lamb for his sins and for the sins of the Aaronic priesthood. Then he entered the Holy of Holies and sprinkled the blood on the "mercy seat" of the Ark of the Covenant, the place from which God displayed mercy to the community of Israel. Combined with this was the offering of two goats, one for God, and one for Azazel. The former atoned for the sins of the people (sins that had been confessed). Then the High Priest placed both of his hands on the Azazel goat, thereby shifting to it the *unconfessed* sins of the people. Soon after, a man from the community led the goat for Azazel out into the desert and abandoned it there. Then the man purified himself by a ritual washing. In this way, the sins of the community were driven to the desert.

The tragedy of Israel's history is that in all the elaboration of ceremonies and festivals, many missed the point of the preparation. Instead of sensing the reality of a coming Christ, they were caught up in their temporal feasts.

Jesus Reinterprets the Feast

Thus, in order to focus the minds of the disciples away from the earthly festival elaboration and onto the eschatological banquet, Jesus reinterpreted Israel's feasts. We can trace His reinterpretation especially in the Passover, for "while they were eating, Jesus took a loaf of bread, and after blessing it, He broke it, gave it to the disciples, and said, 'Take eat; this is My body.' Then He took a cup, and after giving thanks, He gave it to them, saying, 'Drink from it all of you; for this is my blood of the covenant, which is poured out for many for the forgiveness of sins. I tell you, I will never again drink of this fruit of the vine until that day when I drink it new with you, in my Father's kingdom' (Matt. 26:26-29, NRSV).

In the Synoptic tradition and the Gospel of John, the radical reinterpretation of the feast is demonstrated as Jesus turns the Passover into the Last Supper (cf., C. K. Barrett, *The Gospel According to St. John*, pp. 39-41). The actions and words that follow this Last Supper are conditioned by the moment (*Kairos*). "The hour had come" for His body to be "broken" as the true bread, and for His blood to be "spilled" as the true wine.   And as the sun set on Passover Eve, the 14th of Nisan, He would die as the Servant who suffered for humanity.

Having rested in the tomb through the 15th of Nisan, He came forth from the grave on the 16th of Nisan, as **God--The Triumphant Savior**, to complete the establishment of God's Messianic rule.   It is this, for me, that is the ultimate meaning of footwashing.   I participate in it with this attitude:

1.   Preparation for the celebration of The Feast.

2.   Anticipation of the Church's deliverance from the "long night of oppression."

3.   Reassurance that the time of perfect joy in the kingdom of the divine will come.

4.   Inspiration and encouragement of the victory that is to be obtained over the forces of evil.

In a brilliant summary in his book, the _Feast of Fools_, Harvey Cox states that in theology the Christian redefinition of the Messianic hope of Israel provides an excellent example of creative discontinuity. For without the expectations of Israel, Christian Messianism would be meaningless. While Christian Messianism did not fulfill Israel's expectations, it disappointed them, but, at the same time, broadened them.   Then he comments that "Eschatology almost always has this jarring, juxtaposing function. It uses tradition against itself. It recalls the fondly awaited day of the Lord but gives that day a different content..." (pp. 134-135).

This is why I claim that Jesus has declared a feast beyond any feast known to Israel or the history of the Church. That feast will be unobstructed, blissful, ecstatic, and glorious. It is a feast - not of "fools" but - of "the wise." "Those who are wise shall shine like the brightness of the firmament and those who turned many to righteousness as the stars for ever and ever" (Dan.12:3).

Christ is Footwasher No More

The anticipation and rehearsal we have just described tell us that Christ will be footwasher no more, for all through the time of preparation, He has been washing feet. Now, He is both the **Master** and the **Lord** of The Feast. He is the "King of kings" and "Lord of lords." He is the Hospitable One who will be waiting for His friends who already have been cleansed by His sacrifice. As the host of the feast, He epitomizes *hospitality*: "Enter into the joy of your master" (Matt. 25:23), as He summons in His now-purified guests.

The greatest excitement is that "there is room for everyone" (John 14:2). In the *Apocalypse of John* (Rev. 21), it is noted that there are gates on every side of the city - New Jerusalem. And there will be free food, friends, and fellowship, because heaven cannot be heaven otherwise. As the saints enter through the gates, they stand before God the Father, God the Son, and God the Holy Spirit, and they join in the *hallelujahs* -- not at the end of the feast, but before the feast. They have obtained victory over the last enemy - death. The people of God in the time of their preparation have seen signs of victory over death, but now, they have received immortality - full and complete. They are in the presence of the One who cleansed them completely from their sins and made them Children of God. They have on their robes of righteousness, and on their foreheads - the name of Jesus. They can shout in glad *hallelujahs*.

In Chapter 19 of the *Apocalypse of John* (Rev.), we note the progression in the hallelujahs. Four times the hallelujahs

are shouted by the heavenly multitude; once as an affirmation
of the righteous judgement of God (which leads to the salvation
of the righteous); a second time when the enemies of God's
people are judged and destroyed. A third hallelujah is heard
when the twenty-four elders and the four living creatures join
with the saints and even add an _Amen_ to the _Hallelujah_. Then
comes a great big _Hallelujah_. The voices of the great
multitude shout like many thunderpeals, "Hallelujah, for the
Lord God the Almighty reigns! Let us exult and give Him the
glory, for the marriage of the Lamb has come, and his bride
has made herself ready; to her it has been granted to be clothed
with fine linen, bright and pure" - for the linen is the righteous
deeds of the saints.

> There is singing up in heaven
> Such as we have never known.
> Where the angels sing the praises
> Of the Lamb upon the throne;
> Their sweet harps are ever tuneful
> And their voices always clear.
> Oh, that we might be more like them
> While we serve our Master here!
>
> But I hear another anthem,
> blending voices clear and strong:
> "Unto Him who hath redeemed us,
> And hath bought us" is the song;
> We have come thru' tribulations
> To this land so fair and bright,
> In the fountain freely flowing
> He hath made our garments white.
>
> Holy, holy, is what the angels sing,
> And I expect to help them
> Make the courts of heaven ring.

> But when I sing redemption's story,
> They will fold their wings,
> For angels never felt the joys
> That our salvation brings.
> (Johnson Oatman Jr., 1856-1922)

Such a musical noise has never been matched, even by a Davidic choir which led the music at the return of the ark from Philistine country, or at the ascension of the king. It is not just senseless noise, but a wedding song. Judas is not present. Pilate is absent. Caiphas cannot be found. The harlot has been swept away. The accuser of the saints and all manipulative, oppressive forces are no more seen. As many have rightly sensed it in their utopian dreaming, the old order has crumbled. Those who were first will be last (Mk. 10:31). Those who made themselves 'little' will be great (Matt. 18:4). The humble shall be masters (Matt. 5:5), and the oppressed shall be freed. Now the faithful come to their rightful honor. The betrothed, so long waiting amid privation, persecution, and contempt, now becomes a bride of the Lamb. The time of the marriage has at long last arrived, and the grand nuptial banquet begins (cf., J. A. Seiss, *The Apocalypse*, p. 426). All together can now sing in perfect harmony and without a note of discord:

> Crown Him with many crowns,
> The Lamb upon His throne.
> Hark! how the heavenly anthem drowns
> All music but its own!
> Awake my soul and sing
> Of Him who died for thee;
> And hail Him as the matchless King
> Through all eternity.
> (Matthew Bridges, Hymn Writer, 1851)

This is inadequate description but it suffices to state the reality of the _New Community_. In the Upper Room there was an underlayment of disharmony, but we can trust that if Christ washes us, we will have a sense of what it means to be at peace at a banquet. While we wait for the occasion of the "Celebration Feast," we can celebrate our common life in communion with family -- the Family of God, for Judas is with us no more.

Life today is full of pain, poverty, stresses, and pressures, but there is a feast tomorrow, and we can begin to celebrate, for Judas will not be there. It is this one thought that encourages the transcendent vision of community. We do not lose heart when we do not find perfect harmony in this life. We have a precious hope. The idea that we shall not be in "paradise lost," but in "paradise restored," in a place where there will be no conflict between light and darkness, life and death, and love and hatred, is what gives us inspiration to build community here. In the new reality there will be no "afterglow," - but an "everglow," for the feast of life will last and last. As Henry de Fluiter (1872-1970) puts it:

> Water of life there floweth
> Fruit in abundant store;
> Citizens of that country
> Hunger and thirst no more.

The challenge of broken community is at an end, for **Life** and **Light**, and **Peace** and **Joy** are in the midst of us.

SELECTED BIBLIOGRAPHY

Anderson, G., and Stransky, T. *Christ's Lordship and Religious Pluralism*. New York: Orbis Books, 1981.

Anderson, Ray, and Guernsey, Dennis. *On Being Family: A Social Theology of the Family*. Grand Rapids: Eerdmans, 1985.

Andelin, Aubrey. *Man of Steel and Velvet*. Santa Barbara, CA: Pacific Press, 1972.

Arn, Winfred, Charles Arn, and Carroll Nyquist. *Who Cares About Love*. Monrovia, CA: Church Growth, 1988.

Arnot, William. *The Lesser Parables of Our Lord*. Grand Rapids: Kregel, 1981.

Bailey, John. *The Ministry of the Church in the World*. London: Oxford University Press, 1967.

Bakar, David. *And They Took Themselves Wives: The Emergence of Patriarchy in the Western Civilization*. New York: Harper & Row, 1979.

Bakunin, Mikhail. *A Political Philosophy of Bakunin*. G. P. Maximoff, ed. New York: Free Press (Macmillan), 1964.

Balch, David F. *Let Wives Be Submissive: The Domestic Code in I Peter*. New York: Scholars Press, 1981.

Barbeau, Clayton C. *The Head of the Family*. Collegeville, MN: Liturgical Press, 1970.

Barclay, William. *And Jesus Said: A Handbook on the Parables of Jesus*. Philadelphia: Westminster Press, 1970.

-----. *The Letters of James and Peter: The Daily Study Bible Series* Philadelphia: Westminster Press, 1970.

-----. *The Letters to the Philippians, Colossians, and Thessalonians*. Louisville, KY: The Daily Study Bible Series, 1975.

Barrett, C. K. *The Gospel According to St. John*. London: S.P.C.K., 1967.

Barth, Karl. *Church Dogmatics IV:1 The Doctrine of Reconciliation*. Edinburgh: T & T Clark, 1956.

-----. *Church Dogmatics IV:2 The Doctrine of Reconciliation*. Edinburgh: T & T Clark, 1958.

Barth, K. (cont.). *Church Dogmatics IV:3, Part 2. The Doctrine of Reconciliation*. Edinburgh: T & T Clark, 1962.

-----. *The Epistle to the Romans*. E. Hoskyns, ed. London: Oxford University Press, 1933.

Barth, Markus. *The Broken Wall: A Study of the Epistle to the Ephesians*. 1st Edition. Valley Forge, PA: Judson Press, 1959.

Barthes, Roland. *Mythologies*. New York: Hill & Wang, 1972.

Battersby, C. M. "An Evening Prayer," *Rodeheaver's Gospel Solos and Duets, No. 3*. Y. P. Rodeheaver, *et al.*, (eds.). Winona Lake, IN: The Rodeheaver Co., 1966.

Beach, Waldo. *Christian Community & American Society*. Philadelphia: Westminster, 1969.

Bell, Richard. *The Grammar of the Heart: New Essays in Moral Philosophy and Theology*. New York: Harper & Row, 1988.

Bellah, Robert, et al. *Habits of the Heart: Individualism and Commitment in American Life*. New York: Harper & Row, 1985.

Bellet, Maurice. *Facing the Unbeliever*. New York: Herder & Herder, 1967.

Berkouwer, G.C. *Faith and Sanctification*. Grand Rapids: Eerdmans, 1952.

Bernstein, Richard. *New York Times Magazine*, (April 16, 1989): 23-25, 74-76.

Bilezikian, Gilbert. *Beyond Sex Roles: What the Bible Says About a Woman's Place in the Church*. Grand Rapids: Baker Book House, 1985.

Bloesch, Donald G. *Freedom for Obedience*. San Francisco: Harper & Row, 1987.

-----. *The Struggle of Prayer*. Colorado Springs: Helmers and Howard, 1988.

Boff, Leonardo. *Jesus Christ the Liberator: A Critical Christology for Our Time*. New York: Orbis, 1979.

Bonhoeffer, Dietrich. *The Cost of Discipleship*. New York: Macmillan, 1937.

-----. *Letters and Papers from Prison*. New York: Macmillan, 1953.

-----. *Life Together*. New York: Harper & Row, 1954.

Bradford, Charles. "The Church, a Place for Healing," *Adventist Review*, (June 7, 1990):Cover, pp.4,5.

Braine, John. *Room at the Top*. London: Eyre & Spottiswoode, 1957.

Brigg, Charles. (ed.) *The Epistle of St. Peter and St. Jude. ICC.* New York: Charles Scribner's Sons, 1903.

Brown, Charles. *Together Forever: An Invitation to Physical Immortality.* Grand Rapids: Eternal Flame Foundations, 1990.

Brown, Collin. (Gen. ed.) *The New International Dictionary of the New Testament Theology, Vol. 3.* Grand Rapids: Zondervan, 1975.

Bruce, F. F. *New Testament History.* Garden City, NJ: Doubleday, 1972.

Brunner, Emil. *Mediator.* Philadelphia: Westminster Press, 1947.

-----. *The Misunderstanding of the Church.* Philadelphia: Westminster Press, 1951.

Brushaber, George K. "Good Theologians Are Not Enough." *Christianity Today,* 35:10 (Sept. 16, 1991):19f.

Buber, Martin. *I and Thou.* New York: Scribner's, 1970.

-----. *Between Man and Man.* New York: Macmillan, 1965.

_____. *The Way of Response.* Ed. by Norman Glatzer. New York: Schocken Books, 1966.

Bultmann, Rudolf. *Theology of the New Testament.* New York: Scribner's, 1955.

------. *Jesus and the Word.* New York: Scribner's Sons, 1958.

Burne, Eric. *Games People Play.* (The Psychology of Human Relationships). New York: Baltimore Books, 1964.

Buttrick, George. (Gen. ed.) *The Interpreter's Dictionary of the Bible, Vol. VIII, Matthew.* Nashville: Abingdon Press, 1962.

Buscaglia, Leonard. *Love.* New York: Ballantine, 1972.

Campolo, Anthony. *A Reasonable Faith.* Waco, TX: Word Books, 1983.

Chandler, Russ and Sandie. *Your Family, Frenzy or Fun: Creative Family Togetherness.* Los Angeles: Acton House, 1977.

Collins, Gary R. *Beyond Easy Believism.* Waco, TX: Word Books, 1982.

Costa, Roy O. *One Faith, Many Cultures.* New York: Orbis Books, 1988.

Cowden, John B. *St. Paul on Christian Unity.* New York: Fleming Revell, 1923.

Cox, Harvey. *The Feast of Fools.* New York: Harper & Row, 1969.

Crook, Roger. *An Introduction to Christian Ethics.* Englewood Cliffs, NJ: Prentice-Hall, 1990.

Crooker, Joseph H. *The Church of Today.* Cambridge: University Press, 1908.

Crosby, M. "The Dysfunctional Church," *Other Side*, 28 (Jan/Feb 1992):40-41.

Dibbert, Michael. *Spiritual Leadership, Responsible Management.* Grand Rapids: Zondervan, 1989.

Dodd, Charles H. *Apostolic Preaching and Its Development: Three Lectures.* New York: Harper & Row, 1964.

Douglas, Deborah. "Our Service to Others is Hollow, Our Giving to Others is False." *Other Side*, 27 (March-June 1991):12-15.

Driver, Tom. *The Magic of Rituals: Our Need for Liberating Rites That Transform Our Lives & Our Communities.* San Francisco: Harper Collins, 1991.

Dunfee, Susan N. *Beyond Servanthood.* New York: University Press of America, 1989.

Drussel, Enrique. *Ethics and Community.* New York: Orbis Books, 1988.

Eliade, Mircea. *The Sacred and the Profane, The Nature of Religion.* San Diego: Jovanovich, 1959.

Erickson, Millard J. *Christian Theology.* Grand Rapids: Baker Book House, 1983.

Felder, Cain Hope. *Troubling Biblical Waters.* Maryknoll, NY: Orbis Books, 1989.

Fisher, Kathleen. *Women at the Well.* New York: Paulist Press, 1988.

Fiorenza, Elizabeth. *In Memory of Her.* New York: Crossroads, 1990.

Fitch, William. *God and Evil; Studies in the Mystery of Suffering and Pain.* Grand Rapids: Eerdmans, 1967.

Fletcher, Joseph. *Situation Ethics.* Philadelphia: Westminster Press, 1964.

Foster, Charles R. *Teaching in the Community of Faith.* Nashville: Abingdon, 1982.

Foster, Richard. "The Ministry of the Towel: Practicing Love Through Service." *Christianity Today*, (Jan. 7, 1983):18-21.

Fowler, James W. *Stages of Faith.* San Francisco: Harper & Row, 1981.

Getz, Gene. *Sharpening the Focus of Our Church.* Chicago: Moody Press, 1974.

Goode, William J. *The Celebration of Heroes: Prestige As a Social Control System.* Berkeley: University of California Press, 1978.

Gratton, Carolyn. *Trusting: Theory and Practice.* New York: Crossroads/Continuum Publishing Group, 1983.

Greenleaf, Robert K. *Servant Leadership, A Journey into the Nature of Legitimate Power and Greatness.* New York: Paulist Press, 1977.

Grounds, Vernon E. "Called to Be Saints -- Not Well-adjusted Sinners," *Christianity Today,* (January 17, 1986):28.

Grudem, Wayne. "The First Epistle of Peter." *Tyndale New Testament Commentaries.* Leon Morris, gen. ed. Grand Rapids: Eerdmans, 1988.

Gustafson, James. *Treasures In Earthen Vessels.* Chicago: University of Chicago Press, 1985.

Gutierrez, Gustavo. *A Theology of Liberation.* New York: Orbis Books, 1973.

Hadden, Jeffrey. *The Gathering Storm.* New York: Doubleday, 1969.

Hamilton, J.W. *Serendipity.* New York: Revell, 1965.

Hawthorne, Alice. "Whispering Hope." *Seventh-day Adventist Church Hymnal.* Hagerstown, MD: Review & Herald, 1990.

Hestenes, Roberta. *Women and Men in Ministry.* (Collected readings for a course given at Fuller Theological Seminary, Pasadena, CA), 1988.

Herzog, Fredrick. *Liberation Theology.* New York: Seabury Press, 1972.

Hibbert, D. Edmond. "Behind the Word 'Deacon'." *Bibliotheca Sacra,* 140 (April-June 1983):151-162.

Howad, Knee. *Jesus: History an Approach to the Study of the Gospels.* New York: Harcourt, 1990.

Howell, Jane M., and Avolio, Bruce J. "The Ethics of Charismatic Leadership." *The Academy of Management Executive,* 6:2 (May 1992):43.

Hultgreen, Ailand J. "The Johannine Footwashing (John 13:1-11): A Symbol of Eschatological Hospitality." *New Testament Studies,* 28 (1982):539-546.

Hunter, Archibald. *The Work and Words of Jesus.* Philadelphia: SCM Press, 1973.

Innig, Gary. "Called to Serve." *Bibliotheca Sacra,* 140 (Oct-Dec, 1983):335-349.

James, D.A. Dunn. *The Evidence for Jesus.* Philadelphia: Westminster Press, 1985.

James, E. O. *Seasonal Feasts and Festivals.* New York: Barnes & Noble, 1961.

James, William. *The Varieties of Religious Experience.* New York: Cromwell MacMillan, 1961.

Jenkins, Edward Dixon. *Religion Versus Revolution: The Interpretation of the French Revolution.* Austin: Best Print, 1974.

Johnson, James Weldon, (ed.). *The Book of American Negro Poetry.* New York: Harvest/Harcourt Brace Jovanovich, 1950 printing.

Käsemann, Ernst. *The New Testament Questions for Today.* Philadelphia: Fortress Press, 1969.

Kennedy, Robert. *The Search For Community.* Columbia University, New York: Teachers College Press, 1983.

King Jr., Martin Luther. *Where Do We Go From Here: Chaos or Community.* New York: Harper & Row, 1967.

-----. *Strength to Love.* Philadelphia: Fortress Press, 1963.

Klassen, William. *The Forgiving Community.* Philadelphia: Westminster Press, 1966.

Knight, Frank. "Feetwashing" *Encyclopedia of Religion and Ethics.* Edited by James Hastings. New York: Scribner's Sons, 1955.

Kraybill, Donald. *The Upside-Down Kingdom.* Scottdale, PA: Herald Press, 1990.

Lake, Alexander. *Your Prayers Are Always Answered.* New York: Gilbert Press, 1956.

Lewis, C. S. *The Problem of Pain.* New York: Collier Books/Macmillan, 1962.

----. *Spirits in Bondage.* W. Hooper, ed. New York: Harcourt Brace Jovanovich, 1984.

Loades, Ann. (ed.) *Feminist Theology: A Reader.* Louisville, KY: John Knox Press, 1990.

Manual for Ministers. Silver Spring, MD: The General Conference of Seventh-day Adventist, 1990.

Marshall, Katharine. "The Garden Party." *Twelve Short Stories.* Marvin Magalaner and Edmon L. Volpe (eds.). New York: Macmillan, 1969.

Marstin, Ronald. *Beyond Tribal Gods: The Maturing of Faith.* New York: Obris, 1979.

Martin, Ralph. *New Testament Foundations.* Grand Rapids: Eerdmans, 1978.

Maxwell, Graham. *Servants or Friends: Another Look at God.* Redlands, CA: Pineknoll Publications, 1992.

McDonald, H.D. *Forgiveness and Atonement.* Grand Rapids: Baker Books, 1984.

Meier, John P. "The Mission of Christ and His Church." *Studies in Christology and Ecclesiology,* Collegeville, MN: Liturgical Press, 1990.

Menninger, Karl. *Love Against Hate.* New York: Harcourt, Brace & Co., 1942.

-----. *Whatever Became of Sin?* New York: Hawthorn Books, 1973.

Merton, Thomas. *No Man Is An Island.* New York: Doubleday, 1955.

Mitchell, Alan C. "The Social Function of Friendship in Acts 2:44-47 and 4:32-37." *Journal of Biblical Literature,* III:2 (Summer 1992):255.

Moltmann, Jurgen. *Experiences of God.* Philadelphia: Fortress Press, 1980.

-----. *The Church In The Power of The Spirit.* New York: Harper & Row, 1977.

-----. *The Crucified God.* New York: Harper & Row, 1974.

-----. *The Power of The Powerless.* San Francisco: Harper & Row, 1983.

-----. *Theology of Hope.* New York: Harper & Row, 1967.

Moore, Basil. (ed.) *The Challenge of Black Theology in South Africa.* Atlanta: John Knox Press, 1974.

Morris, Leon. *Testaments of Love: A Study of Love in the Bible.* Grand Rapids: Eerdmans, 1981.

-----. *The First & Second Epistles to the Thessalonians.* Grand Rapids: Eerdmans, 1959.

-----. *The New Century Bible Commentary: Galatians.* Grand Rapids: Eerdmans, 1981.

Moule, C.F.D. "The Individualism of the Fourth Gospel." *N.T.5,* (1962):174.

Muggerige, Malcolm. *Something Beautiful for God - Mother Theresa of Calcutta.* London: Collins & Sons Ltd., 1971.

Myers, Allen C. *The Eerdmans Bible Dictionary.* Revised Edition. Grand Rapids: Eerdmans, 1987.

Nelson, C. Ellis. *Where Faith Begins.* Atlanta: John Knox Press, 1971.

Nelson, J. Robert. *Criterion for the Church.* New York: Abingdon, 1962.

Neuhaus, Richard. (ed). "Confession, Conflict and Community: Ethics and the Human Community." *New Testament Studies*, 28 (1986):539-546.

Niebuhr, Reinhold. *Beyond Tragedy*. New York: Scribners, 1937.

-----. *Justice and Mercy*. New York: Harper & Row, 1974.

-----. *The Nature and Destiny of Man*. Vol.1. New York: Scribners, 1941.

-----. *The Nature and Destiny of Man*. Vol.2. New York: Scribners, 1943.

Niebuhr, Richard. *Radical Monotheism and Western Culture with Supplementary Essays*. New York: Harper & Row, 1943.

Noyce, Gaylord. *Pastoral Ethics*. Nashville: Abingdon Press, 1988.

Oates, Stephen B. *Let The Trumpet Sound: The Life of Martin Luther King, Jr*. New York: Harper & Row, 1982.

Oldham, Dale. Gaither, Gloria and William. "I Believe in a Hill Called Mount Calvary." Grand Rapids: *Singspiration of Zondervan Corporation*, 1968.

Palmer, Parker J. *The Company of Strangers*. New York: Crossroads, 1981.

Parks, Robert and E. W. Burgess. "The City: Suggestions for the Investigation of Human Behavior in the Urban Environment." *The City*. Chicago: University of Chicago Press, (1967):40.

Peck, Scott. *The Different Drum*. New York: Simon & Schuster, 1987.

Peters, Tom. *Megatrends 2000:The Next Ten Years*. London: Sidgwick & Jackson, 1990.

Quebedeaux, Richard. *By What Authority: The Rise of Personality Cults in American Christianity*. New York: Harper & Row, 1982.

The Random House Dictionary of the English Language. 2nd ed. 1987.

Richards, Lawrence O. *The Theology of Church Leadership*. Grand Rapids: Zondervan, 1980.

Richardson, Alan. *An Introduction to the Theology of the New Testament*. New York: Harper & Row, 1958.

Richmond, Kent. "A Secret Bond of Caring." *The Christian Ministry*, 1:128 (January 1979):0-10.

Richter, George. *Die Fusswoschung im Johannese Evangelium Geschichte Ihrer Deutung*. Pustet: Regensburg, 1967.

Robinson, J.A.T. *Jesus and His Coming*. 2nd ed. Philadelphia: Westminster Press, 1979.

Rosado, Caleb. *What Is God Like?* Washington, D.C.: Review & Herald, 1988.

Rossi, Andrew. "Reciprocity and Interpretation: Theological Meditation on Christian Community." *Epiphany*, 11 (Summer 1991):77-86.

Russell, Letty M. "Good Housekeeping," in *Feminist Theology: A Reader*. Ann Loades, editor. Philadelphia: Westminster Press, 1981.

-----. *Growth in Partnership.* Philadelphia: Westminster Press, 1981.

Sampley, J. Paul. *And The Two Shall Become One Flesh.* Cambridge: The University Press, 1971.

Seiss, J. A. *The Apocalypse.* Grand Rapids: Zondervan, 1900.

Semedes, Lewis. "Forgiveness, the Power to Change the Past." *Christianity Today*, (Jan. 7, 1983):22-26.

-----. "Preaching to Ordinary People." *Christianity Today*, (Fall, 1983):114-119.

Seventh-day Adventist Church Manual. Issued by the General Conference of Seventh-day Adventists (revised 1986), Silver Springs, Maryland.

Soelle, Dorothee. *Beyond Mere Obedience.* New York: Pilgrim Press, 1982.

-----. *Choosing Life.* Philadelphia: Fortress Press, 1981.

Spohn, William C. *What Are They Saying About Scripture and Ethics?* New York: Paulist Press, 1984.

Stewart, James. *The Life and Teaching of Christ.* Nashville: Abingdon Press, 1957.

Stone, Ronald H. (ed.) *Liberation and Change.* Atlanta: John Knox Press, 1972.

Stott, John R.W. *Understanding Christ.* Grand Rapids: Zondervan, 1981.

Swindoll, Charles R. *Living On The Ragged Edge.* Waco, TX: Word Books, 1985.

Tarnas, Richard. *The Passion of the Western Mind.* New York: Harmony Books, 1991.

Tillich, Paul. *Love, Power and Justice.* London: Oxford University Press, 1960.

-----. *The New Being.* New York: Scribners, 1955.

de Tocqueville, Alexis. *Democracy in America.* Trans. by Henry Reeve. Cambridge, MA: Seren & Francis, 1862.

Tschachert, Paul. "Footwashing." *The New Schaff Herzog*

Tschachert, Paul.   "Footwashing."   *The New Schaff Herzog Encyclopedia of Religious Knowledge, Vol. VI.* Grand Rapids: Baker Book House, 1977.

Van Beeck, Frans Josef. *Christ Proclaimed.* New York: Paulist Press, 1979.

Van Kaam, Adrian. *Looking for Jesus.* Dansville, NY: Dimension Books, 1987.

Washington, James. *A Testament of Hope: The Essential Writings and Speeches of Martin Luther King, Jr.* San Francisco: Harper Collins, 1986.

Weber, Max. *Economy and Society: An Outline of Interpretative Sociology.* Guenther Roth and Claus Wittick, eds. New York: Harper & Row, 1968.

Wesley, John.   *The Works of John Wesley.* Vol.6.   London: Conference Office, 1809.

White, Ellen. *The Acts of the Apostles.* Boise, Idaho: Pacific Press, c. 1911.

-----. *The Desire of Ages.* Boise, Idaho: Pacific Press, c. 1898.

-----. " Ministry." *Signs of the Times,* Vol.26:20 (May 16,1900):1-2.

White, James. "When Jesus Christ Was Here." *Hymns for God's Peculiar People.* Printed by Richard Oliphant, 1949.

White, R. E. O.   *The Night He Was Betrayed.*   Grand Rapids: Eerdmans, 1982.

Williams, Cecil, & Rebecca Laird. *No Hiding Place.* San Francisco: Harper, 1992.

Willimon, William H. "Living by the Word: Thick Water." *Christian Century,* v108, 12 (April 10, 1941):B95f.

Wilson, Bryan R. "New Images of Christian Community." *Oxford Illustrated History of Christianity.* J. McManus (ed.) (1990):572-601.

Yorke, Gosnell. *The Church As The Body of Christ.* Lanham, MD: University Press of America, 1991.

Yoder, John. *The Politics of Jesus.* Grand Rapids: Eerdmans, 1972.

SUBJECT INDEX

ABOUT THE AUTHOR.....

D. Robert Kennedy is an Associate Professor of Religion at Atlantic Union College in South Lancaster, Massachusetts. He is a trained minister of the Gospel and has spent more than 23 years working in various areas of church ministry. For several years he was a speaker on the "What God Did for Humanity" TV program in New York City. He is a people-oriented person and takes time to comfort and encourage many persons in their times of frustration and suffering. Aside from being a religion scholar, Dr. Kennedy does gardening and woodwork to create variety in his life. Even though he speaks of himself mostly as a Pastor and Teacher, Dr. Kennedy is an effective consultant in Multicultural and Human Relations issues. His doctoral and post-doctoral work have taken him into such areas of study as Christian Theology, Religion, and Education. He is a teaching scholar with the American Academy of Religion Lilly Foundation Workshop. He has published several magazine and journal articles and also a book on *Marriage, Divorce and Connected Issues (as viewed from Paul in 1 Corinthians 7:1-16)*. He is married to Seslie June Barham, and they have three sons, Robert, Leighton, and Sheldon. Presently, Dr. Kennedy has been spending much time in the study of the impact of the Holy Spirit on the life of the church, and is working on a manuscript called *The Politics of the Spirit*.